Something's Up with Dad

Nitsan Tal

Production by eBookPro Publishing
www.ebook-pro.com

SOMETHING'S UP WITH DAD
Nitsan Tal

Copyright © 2025 Nitsan Tal

ISBN 9798288187919

Something's Up with Dad

*The Highs and Lows of Growing Up
with a Bipolar Father*

NITSAN TAL

*"But if love is not the cure,
it certainly can act as a very strong medicine."*

— Kay Redfield Jamison,
An Unquiet Mind: A Memoir of Moods and Madness

For Dad.

Contents

Decision

March 2015

I look at the clock on the wall. It's already four. Shit, I was supposed to be at work hours ago. I have to call. I manage to get my phone out of my handbag, but I can't find the contacts. Nothing looks familiar. It's all a jumble of icons I don't recognize. I decide to just hurry there. I get into an elevator, The metallic surface is entirely smooth, with no buttons and the elevator is speeding up. My phone rings in my hand, but I can't figure out how to answer it.

I wake up. For a second, I think my phone's ringing but decide it was just in the dream. Turning over, the clock on my night table glows 5:23 a.m. Then the faint ringing resumes; this time I'm sure it's real. I lurch out of bed and race down the hallway, my aching morning joints begging to slow down while my body is being flooded with adrenalin, who could be calling me so early? My husband's in China on business, supposed to fly back today, so it's probably not him. I find the cordless handset on the kitchen counter just as the answering machine picks up.

"Hello?"

"Nits, it's me," My sister, from Israel. Something's wrong.

"Hey, what's...?"

"Dad fell and hit his head... bad."

"Is he Okay?"

"No..."

"Where…"

"Listen," she interrupts me, and then continues without stopping, "I'm at the hospital. We've been trying to reach you. Dad fell on the stairs. He suffered severe head trauma and has intracranial bleeding. The doctor says that if they take him to surgery now, they might be able to save his life but his chances aren't very good. If he survives, he'll need months of rehab in the hospital and will most likely be debilitated for the rest of his life. If they don't do anything, he'll die within a day or two. We need to decide."

I'm about to protest that I can't make such a decision on the spot when I realize that I already know the answer.

"He wouldn't want to live like that… He hates hospitals." I say. "What do you think?"

"That's what I told the doctor, but I had to ask you first."

Tortoise Ride

1970

One of my earliest memories is of a trip to the Tel Aviv Zoo with my father. I was probably 4 years old; a skinny girl with short black hair and narrow green eyes. Photos of the zoo from that period reveal dusty, run-down enclosures fenced with chicken-wire held in place with unpainted splintering wood frames. Incarcerated animals pace the tiny bare-bone kennels and look as dull and drab as the sandy ground.

As a little girl, I didn't notice all those details. I was just excited to be on an unexpected day trip with my dad, walking next to him; my left hand hugged in his, my right hand sticky, holding a sweating lemon ice-pop. We stopped by the tortoise habitat. It had a dirt floor surrounded by a low iron railing. Four slow-moving giants were dragging themselves around. One of them got close to the fence and my dad, with half a smile, asked me, "Look, he's coming close, do you want to ride him?"

"Can I?" I looked at him, amazed.

He lifted me over the rail and placed me on the tortoise's back. My legs straddling the warm, smooth shell on both sides, my sandaled feet a good 10 inches from the floor. It was fun! I rode it for a couple of minutes until I noticed it was walking toward their "house," a concrete structure with an arched opening, just slightly taller than the animals themselves. I visualized the tortoise squeezing into the hole while I'm being shoved off his back onto the ground. I was still considering my options when my dad noticed my distress, hopped over the fence, picked me up, and extracted me from the pen. Just then, a zoo security guard noticed us and came running, yelling, "Sir, sir, what are you doing? Get out of there!"

My dad mumbled a half-hearted apology, and we scurried away, laughing.

Eulogy

March 2015

I hung up the phone with my sister and went to get my wallet. I called the airline number on the back of the Frequent Flyer card and asked to book the next available flight to Israel. The sales agent was polite, slowly listing the available flights. He said there were no direct flights from Newark until the next day, but if I'd like to fly out that night, there were several options through Europe. He took his time quoting the prices for economy and business, and I barely held back from shouting at him, "I don't care about the price; my father is dying." Instead, I asked him which flight arrived in Israel the earliest, hoping to make it before my dad passed away. I booked a 6 p.m. flight with a layover in Germany. It was scheduled to land in Israel by 3 p.m. the next day.

Next, I dialed my husband's cell. The call went directly to voicemail. Shit. His plane was already in the air and scheduled to land after my departure. I tried to leave a message: "Odedi, I have to go to Israel, my…" then I started sobbing, unable to finish the sentence. I hung up, calmed myself down, blew my nose, and tried again. I believe the second message was even shorter than the first but ended up just the same way. I decided that a text message would be a better way to convey the pertinent information, hoping he would see it before listening to the unintelligible voice messages.

It was only 6:15; too early to call any of my friends or wake up the kids, so I made myself an Americano and sat in the kitchen, staring at my mug. A thought circled in my head like an angry bee: Did I just kill my father?!

After a short layover in Germany, I boarded the flight to Tel Aviv. I was just about to turn on flight mode when my sister's name flashed on the phone's screen.

"Nits? He died. A few minutes ago." I took a deep breath. So, this is it. I knew it was coming, but now it was real.

"OK. I'm on the plane. I'll call you when we land." What else was there to say?

"Are you OK?"

"No. You?"

"Not really."

But we both knew we'd be fine.

"There's one more thing," she said. "The hospital is asking if we'd like to see the body. They'll keep him somewhere until you arrive. Do you?"

"No. What for?" I said, struggling to close the seat belt buckle with the one hand that wasn't holding the phone. I'd hoped to arrive before he died; to be able to hold his hand and talk to him one last time, but I did not want to see his body. I didn't want that to be my last memory of him.

A flight attendant with a stern expression signaled me to turn my phone off, and I raised my hand in apology.

The poor German guy sitting next to me noticed me crying and politely asked if I was okay. I contemplated an honest answer, but didn't see the point in that either, so I just nodded.

* * *

The next day I woke up from a deep sleep to the sound of my alarm. The events of the last couple of days trickled slowly into my consciousness; I was at my mom's, my dad was dead, this afternoon was the funeral, and I'm expected to talk.

On the way to the bathroom, I turned on the kettle, and while the French press was brewing, I began changing into my jogging gear. I rummaged through my luggage, searching with mounting annoyance for my running socks, arm strap, and earphones. I found nothing I was looking for. Irked, I emptied the entire content on the floor and finally found what I needed. I left the mess and stepped outside into stifling humidity. Within minutes I was drenched in sweat. I forgot how hot it gets in Israel, even in March.

I ran with my eyes on the ground, skipping over the cracks in the uneven sidewalk, and almost bumped into a trash can standing in the middle of the road. A dog came charging out of a house, barking at me. What's wrong with the people here?

I tried to think about the eulogy. What could I say about him? That he barely had any friends? That his own family preferred to keep him locked away? That mental illness screwed up his life? He didn't have any outstanding achievements; the likes of which people exaggerate at funerals.

I pushed on, noticing that the little fairytale house on the corner was gone and the wildflower beds around it destroyed. In its place stood a skeleton of new construction, the yard littered by debris.

An old lady sauntered with a walker on the path. I said, "Excuse me," and when I saw that she scooted a bit to the left, proceeded to pass her on her right. She changed direction last minute, and I almost knocked her over. I stopped and apologized profusely, but she just smiled warmly, patted me on my sticky arm, and said, "I'm sorry, I forgot my hearing aid. Go on."

I reached a newly repaired stretch of road. There was nobody else there, and I could charge ahead. A breeze came from the valley, mixed with a faint scent of pine trees and wild herbs, cooling me down.

Maybe I could say something about his phenomenal memory

or his love of films and books? I would definitely have to acknowledge the disease that gripped and shaped his life.

My running app announced in a cheerful robotic voice, "Great job! You have reached your goal of 3 miles." Feeling energized, I decided to go a bit further.

Back at the house I found paper and a pen in the usual place, a wooden box by the phone, hand-decorated with colorful tiny flowers by my mom during a long-ago wood-painting phase.

A second glass of tap water beside me, I sat down to write an outline of the eulogy before it dissipated.

Like trying to retell a dream, there's an elusive quality to ideas that seem so coherent during a run. It takes a while to sort them out. Finally satisfied with the piece, I left it on the table and hit the shower.

Running clothes under one arm, I clumsily fought with the flimsy laundry rack, trying to stabilize its uneven legs on the patio stones without trampling any of my mom's potted flowers. I finally managed to get them hung to dry, and when I bent down to pluck a sock from the Begonia plant, I heard footsteps approaching.

"Hey, Nits," my sister said. We hugged briefly "How are you?" she asked. Inside, I made coffee, and we sat at the kitchen table to talk. I had zillions of questions about the events of the last two days, but first we had to go over funeral details.

I already knew that my dad's kibbutz would take care of the practicalities; the coffin, picking up the body from the hospital, designating the burial spot, and digging the grave. It was up to us to decide if we wanted to talk or read something, and we could also choose a song to play at the end of the ceremony.

"A song? Like what?" I asked. I had a hard time thinking of something appropriate.

"Let's Google it," she said.

I typed "Song for funeral or memorial service" and got some

hits. Most of the suggested pieces were about young, fallen soldiers. After all, we were in Israel, the land of perpetual military conflicts. A couple of songs were more general. We played a few on YouTube, feeling them out. We ruled out anything about angels and vetoed stuff like: "I did it my way." How do you mourn a person who lived a mostly lonely life, who we let go, let die because we thought it was in his best interest?

My sister suggested the song "One Human Tapestry." We read the words aloud.

"When I'm gone, something inside you
will die with me.
When you're gone, something inside me
will die with you.
For we are all made as one human tapestry.
And if someone is missing, if someone is leaving,
something will die in us."

Performed by Chava Alberstein, a singer Dad liked, we decided it was perfect. It acknowledges the grief of losing someone without making them a hero or a saint.

* * *

The kibbutz cemetery sits on a beautiful spot overlooking the Jezreel Valley. In March, the valley is a patchwork of rectangular fields in shades of green, a lattice of rich brown roads running between them. The graveyard itself drapes over the hill in an irregular shape; rows of headstones lay under a canopy of pine trees, pine needles covering the ground, and the graves that have not been visited lately. I was surprised at the large crowd awaiting the ceremony. Gratitude for my friends and remote family was mixed with a cynical "nice of you to visit him now" feeling toward the kibbutz members and childhood friends who had come from all over the country.

Among the people who came to give their condolences was Noah, my father's cousin, easily recognized by his long white beard and large black Kippah. A former air force pilot, he fell captive by the Syrian army in 1973, and when he returned home from a hellish eight months as POW, he found God and became the only orthodox member of our extended family. After greeting me in the traditional "May you never know sorrow again," he asked if we would allow him to say Kaddish, a prayer said by a son on his father's grave according to Judaism. Being that my family is secular, we do not usually say prayers at a funeral. We thanked him for asking and told him we would be honored.

We gathered by the open grave, and four kibbutz members carried the casket and lowered it to the ground. One by one, people stepped up to talk or read.

Noah said the Kaddish, my aunt Leah, the designated family historian, read a short chronology of Dad's life, a sterile version of major life events. She then invited me to speak.

Paper in my right hand, a tissue ready in my left, I stepped up to the microphone.

"Dad had a phenomenal memory. He remembered everything. Dates and places, stories, and people. He remembered all the used cars I've ever owned and could list the mechanical troubles I had with each one.

He loved films and knew the names of all the actors. When he was in a good mood, we could have a conversation about a movie he recently watched and who was in it, then progress to listing other movies they were in, and who else was there. We could cover a significant chunk of Hollywood's history in one phone call. He also loved books by Lawrence Sanders and Mira Magen.

And there was his illness, always looming as a threat.

Dalia and I knew from a very early age that Dad had bipolar disorder and what it meant. Everyone who knew us knew about it too. We never felt like we had to hide it or be embarrassed about it.

We learned to recognize the signs of an episode early and prepare. We helped as much as we could, but mainly we tried hard to make him feel that, first and foremost, he was our father and we loved him. We knew he loved us.

Dad always bought us sweets and gifts, but his most significant gift to us was that we learned to care and respect every human being, no matter their circumstances."

I moved back to my previous spot, next to my mom, the tissue in my hand surprisingly dry.

My sister read next, and then my stepfather, Dubi, who thanked Dad for his generosity and kindness, which allowed us all to be in good relations. Two of my sister's children followed and then others. Again, I was surprised when more than a few people I didn't recognize told stories about Dad that I'd never heard.

I was wrapped in thought when the first lines of the song punched me in the gut.

"When I'm gone, something inside you will die with me.

When you're gone, something inside me will die with you."

In an instant, I found myself sobbing uncontrollably, almost howling, nose dripping and all. My mom next to me was quick with the tissue, and as I got a grip on myself, I whispered to her, "Who the heck chose that song?"

That evening, back in my mom's kitchen, we rehashed the day's events. Mom explained who some of the people were that Dalia and I didn't recognize or that looked familiar but couldn't place.

She told us that after the funeral, a few old friends voiced surprise at the love and devotion Dalia and I expressed in our eulogies.

"Seriously?" I said, "What did they expect?"

"You'd be surprised," Mom said, her eyes moist, "how often I hear about children who distance themselves from a mentally ill parent."

That night, lying in bed, a mixture of jet lag and thoughts kept me from falling asleep. I thought about Dad and wondered if I could still tell his story even though he was gone. I got into filmmaking a few years ago and had been thinking about making a documentary about him. I've been telling bits and pieces of his story to people all my life, but I knew there was a lot of information missing in order to paint a more complete picture. I'd asked him if I could interview him on camera whenever I visited Israel and he agreed. But because he was depressed most of the time, we only managed to really film on two occasions. We didn't get far, and now he was gone.

At the funeral I realized that many people knew him and remembered anecdotes and events he was involved in; maybe I'd be able to piece together his life story from my memories and from theirs.

The question of why I'd want to do it didn't come up. Anthropologists speculate extensively about the origin and evolutionary benefits of storytelling. It is, after all, a major component of human experience; from oral, to written, to filmed, to posted. I read articles and while some of them make sense, none of them capture the enjoyment of reading a good story or the satisfaction of telling one. I've always been a story consumer and teller, and now I fell asleep resolving to try and tell his story by interviewing people who knew him.

Headstone

March 2015

I stayed in Israel for a week following my father's funeral. A few days after I returned to my home in New Jersey, my sister called. "Hi, what's up? How's your jet lag?"

"Getting there, almost back to normal."

"Listen, the guy who's making the headstone said that because of the type of ground at the cemetery, we need to wait 3 months for the dirt to settle before putting it up." That meant we wouldn't be able to do the unveiling ceremony 30 days after our father's passing, as was the Jewish custom.

"OK, I'll plan for June then."

"You're coming?"

"Yes. I want to be there and maybe also start interviewing people who knew him."

"For the film? I didn't know if you were serious. Who do you want to interview?"

"I don't know. We can start with family. Let's say, Grandma Deborah and Mom. Who else?"

"Do you think Yair and Ruth will agree to talk?" She was referring to my dad's siblings, with whom we had some disagreements over the years.

"We can ask," I said. Already dreading the asking part.

"How about Professor Ginath? I have his number. He was very helpful a few years ago when we asked him for the medical records." Now I was feeling intrigued. The thought of meeting

Ginath, a mythological creature in our family's history, excited the documentarian in me.

"Will you be able to take time off and join me?" I asked her. I'll feel more comfortable if she comes along.

"I think so. Maybe not the whole week but a few days. Oh, and there's one more thing. We need to decide what to write on the headstone. Other than the obvious, you know, name and dates. Do you want to write something else?"

"Maybe a quote from a poem?"

"Like...?"

"I don't know. Something that will acknowledge the disease but also our love?"

The next day I texted her:

THROUGH PEAKS AND VALLEYS, WE ALWAYS LOVED YOU.

THROUGH PEAKS AND VALLEYS, WE ALWAYS LOVED YOU AND FOREVER WILL She replied.

That's what's written on my father's headstone.

Beginnings

1962-63

On a warmish Thursday afternoon at the end of December, Alona Goldshmidt sat in her dorm room writing a letter to a friend in the army. Albert, her Eurasian Jay pet birdling landed on her desk, vying for her attention. He grabbed the corner of the letter in his little beak and tore a small piece off. Alona tried to shoo him away gently, but he kept coming back.

A few weeks earlier, someone at the college found the bird, weak and unable to fly, and Alona, who had some experience in taking care of abandoned nestlings, nursed him back to health with the help of her roommates. They named him Albert after A. Einstein because he was smart. Alona and her friends, with the motherly instincts of young women, tolerated his flying around the room, leaving whitish drops of poop everywhere, including their shoulders and hair. She guiltily got up to put him back in his cage when Judith, her roommate, came rushing through the open door, breathless and excited; they were invited on an over-night trip to the South, to the Judean Desert. Someone had arranged for three off-road vehicles, and she was told she could bring friends.

Alona hesitated. She was behind on her homework and planned to catch up on the weekend, but the prospect of a rustic trip to the desert, especially in the winter, after a bit of rain had teased out fields of tiny flowers was too exciting to refuse. She put aside the pen and paper and began to pack.

She was nineteen, studying for a teacher's certificate at a small college in Northern Israel. It was a three-year program, and she was completing it prior to enlisting in the Israeli army for the mandatory two-year service. She liked the idea of being a teacher and by getting her certificate before the service it was ensured that she would serve as a soldier-teacher and not in some boring secretarial job, like most female soldiers did at the time.

The guys picked them up at dawn on Friday. Alona climbed up into the back, brushed away some dust from the seat with her hand and sat down behind the driver, a guy with curly rust-colored hair and sun burned nape. Judith sat up front.

Riding in an open vehicle was exhilarating. The rush of wind on her body inflated and deflated her t-shirt and small strands of hair that escaped the braid, flew around her face. The gusting of air and roaring of the engine during the drive on the highway didn't allow for conversation, so instead they sang old folk songs everybody knew. Before going off-road, they stopped at a gas station, and Alona undid her long black braid so she could comb out the dirt and sand before braiding it again. Mission accomplished, she looked up and saw that the red-headed driver had been watching her.

"You have a good voice." he said. "Do you like to sing?"

He was tall and wide shouldered; his curly hair the color of dry wheat fields at sunset.

She blushed so deeply her light freckles almost disappeared. She didn't think anybody could hear her singing over the racket of the engine and the wind.

"I do. Do you?"

"Yes, sometimes, although I would have preferred listening to music instead. I wish we could get some classical music on the radio out here. I'm Saul, by the way. What's your name?"

"Alona."

On subsequent stops they talked some more. He told her he was from Ein Arava, a kibbutz only 6 miles from the village she grew up in. He was also taking a gap year before joining the army, working as a youth group leader. He asked if she knew the names of some desert flowers and she did. It's the kind of thing you learn in teachers' college. He said he liked nature but didn't know too many names, so every time they saw a new species she pointed it out and told him what she knew about it.

The next morning, he invited her to sit next to him in the passenger seat. The drive on the rocky desert roads was slower, so they could talk to each other.

"Are you girls in a hurry to go back? Do you mind if we stop on the way home in Beer-Sheva to buy something?" He asked at some point.

"Sure. That's cool."

"I need to buy a present for my little brother. I promised my dad I'd take care of him tomorrow morning, so I want to bring him something."

"You take care of your brother? Don't you live in a kibbutz? I thought kids on a kibbutz lived in the Children's House?" Alona asked.

"Yes...Em..." he hesitated. "It's... well... he isn't totally OK."

"Your brother? What's wrong with him?"

He told her his brother was born with brain damage, and his father, a man with strong moral convictions, insisted the family care for the child and not place him in a home.

"Is it hard to take care of him?" She asked.

"I don't mind. I love him. He doesn't really respond to anything, he doesn't smile or play, but I take him for walks, and sometimes I think he's starting to notice things. I want to buy him one of those toys you can hang from a stroller."

Alona looked away, pretending to notice something in the distance and quickly wiped her eyes.

"Are you okay?" he asked.

"Some sand got into my eyes but it's out now. I'm fine."

A few days later, Saul came to visit the college. At first Alona thought he was there for someone else, one of the other girls, but it turned out he was there for her. They went for a walk in the fields and talked. That was their first date.

That year they spent a lot of time together. They often went on nature hikes with some friends and camped out overnight in sleeping bags.

In the summer, it was time for both of them to enlist in the army. He joined Sayeret Shaked, an elite unit of border security stationed in the south of Israel. She was sent to the North to teach new immigrants housed in temporary settlements. Now they could only see each other infrequently.

1/10/1964

My beloved Alona,

It's Friday night, I'm sitting on my bed writing to you. Quiet songs are playing on the radio (I'd prefer classical music, but I can't argue with the ignorant majority). I long for you more than ever, my faraway girl. I miss talking to you, being next to you. Did you get my letter from Monday?

Last night we went on a 45-mile trek, from 3 in the afternoon to 6 this morning and then slept only three and a half hours before waking up for formation. I'm exhausted, but I still wanted to write you a few words. It rained last week, and the desert was so beautiful after the rain. Little flowers are coming out, and I'm trying to remember the names that you taught me. I wish you were here to see it. Your last letter made me so sad. You sound lonely. I hope you'll get to teach the 1st-grade class. I'm sure you'll be a great teacher. I love to hear how motivated you are to be the best teacher you can be. Never give up.

Wait for my phone call next Saturday at 8 p.m. OK?

Yours,

Saul.

First Warning

1964-7

After a year in the army, Alona requested to be transferred closer to Saul's base. She liked her service and felt she was doing an essential job, but she also wanted to be able to see him more often. When her transfer request was denied, they decided to get married. Married women are automatically discharged from the Israeli army.

They had a small wedding at her parents' house, and after she was discharged, she found a job as a teacher on a kibbutz near his base. It was a good year. They couldn't live together, but he was able to visit her frequently, and she got permission from his commander to visit him at the base.

When Saul was discharged from the army, they moved to the moshav (a village-like community where resources and income are shared) where she grew up. Since the moshav had paid for her studies, she was expected to go back and teach there for a couple of years. She taught elementary school and he worked in agriculture. I was born in April 1966.

In June of 1967, my dad was drafted to fight In the Six Day War. He fought in Jerusalem, and his unit suffered many casualties. One of his closest friends was killed. Back at home, he had a hard time getting over his melancholia, more so than other young men who came back from the war. At the time, Mom perceived it as a normal reaction, especially for someone who was so sensitive. Later, she thought this may have been a first warning of what was to come.

Caricatures

June 2015

I turned into the road leading to "Shaar Haamakim." I'd never been to this kibbutz, but still, it felt familiar. The heavy gate at the entrance, the guard's *Budke* (Yiddish for guard booth) deserted during the morning hours, the green Lantana bushes dotted with red and yellow flowers, the warm scent of cow manure.

Yoav waited for me at the visitors' gravel parking lot, seated in his club car, a popular transportation device among older kibbutz members. He stood up; a tall, wiry guy with a full head of white hair, and offered his hand for a shake. "I can't say who you look like," he said, thoughtfully studying my face. "You're pretty like Alona, but there's also something of Saul...."

We loaded my photography equipment into the back of the cart and began the short ride to his home.

"It was lovely talking to Alona the other day," he said. "How long are you staying?"

"I'll be here for a week. The headstone unveiling ceremony is on Friday, and I'm filming a few interviews."

It was 3 months after my father passed away. When I talked to my mom about the visit, she mentioned Yoav as someone who knew Dad and might be willing to share some stories. At that point, I had a very short list of people to talk to, and my plan was to cast a wider net to see what I could catch. Anyone who knew my dad was of interest. Yoav had time and was eager to talk, so he was first on my list.

He showed me around his small apartment, and I suggested the kitchen table for the interview because the room had a large window, filtering in ample natural light. The background of melon-yellow kitchen cabinets wasn't the most attractive, but since I didn't bring any lighting equipment, it seemed the best option. I was nervous. I had only been working with video for a couple of years and wasn't entirely confident in my technical abilities. Telling myself no one else has to see it if I mess up only helped a little. While I was setting up, Yoav went to change into a more "presentable" shirt (I suggested a neutral shade with no logos). He returned, holding two books.

"Here, come look at these," he said.

One was an old self-adhesive photo album; the other was a light blue hardcover sketchbook. Yoav explained that he drew caricatures in that booklet and wanted to show me the ones he sketched during their army service together.

"Let's start, and I'll show you the relevant ones as we go," he suggested as he sat down.

I connected him to the neck mic and asked him to count to three a few times. When I was satisfied with the sound level, I pressed record.

"So let me tell you how I met Saul," Yoav opened without waiting for my question.

"I got to the MEPS (Military Entrance Processing Center) with no clue about what I wanted to do in the army. They told me there's this commando unit, Shaked, and do you want to try out. I said fine. They put down my name and told me the unit's commander would come later to interview us. He was a Bedouin IDF officer who drafted mostly kibbutz members. We waited there, and he came; his Hebrew name was Amos Yarkoni; of course, that wasn't his real name. He had an Arab name, but he never used it. Anyway, he asked each of us a few questions; it went fairly quickly. I don't think it was really about what you answered but more about his impression of you. I guess the same way he had a good eye for tracking footprints, he could also tell things about a person. Right on the spot, he told eight of us, including Saul, that we were in."

Yoav opened the blue sketchbook and flipped through it. When he found what he was looking for, he held it up to the camera. It was a caricature drawn with a black Sharpie on an off-white page. In it, four soldiers are standing in the foreground, and a row of stick figures are marching in the back. Of the two soldiers on the right, one looks angry, and the other confused. The two soldiers on the left are surrounded by a halo and look happy. One of the joyful soldiers has a mustache and red hair. It's the only part of the drawing that was colored in. "This here is Saul, with the red hair," explained Yoav. "That's him and another friend – proud they had been selected for the unit."

"Was Shaked such a big deal?" I asked. Other units were considered "Elite" in my time, but I've never heard of Shaked. Dad would sometimes mention it in passing, connected to a person he knew back then, but never went into details.

"Oh, yes, it had a reputation as being one of the finest, most selective reconnaissance units. It was rumored to run an especially rigorous training regimen, and its activity was shrouded in secrecy."

There is no higher acclaim for a young Israeli man than being selected for a prestigious army position. It's the equivalent of an American high-school senior getting into Stanford or being recruited as a division 1 team quarterback.

Israeli teens prepare for the army and fantasize about it for years before being drafted. Names and rumors of elite units are whispered in awe, and a person's military background follows him as a badge of honor (or mark of shame) for years to come. I could only imagine how my dad felt that day, a combination of pride and dread. What a contrast to the person I knew, who had no higher education or career credentials to flaunt, no possessions or achievement to showcase in our increasingly judgmental and materialistic society.

"Before joining the unit, we had to pass basic training and the paratroopers' course. Both were hard. The goal, especially in the paratroopers, was to bring you to the point where nothing scares you, and you're sure you can do anything, including going for days without sleep. You end up believing it all.

On our last day, two guys came with a vehicle to take us to the unit, and the first thing they said to us was, "Oh boy you have no idea what they're gonna do to you there." Like we weren't already scared enough. When we got to the base, they placed us, the eight new guys, in one room in the barracks. Here." Yoav held up another drawing. It was sketched in the same style as the first one and showed eight guys in a room, each on a single bed. And again, the only part colored in was my dad's hair. The title on top read: Presenting the Renowned Room.

"That's the eight of us, the August 1963 draftees to the Shaked Unit. This is Roni Shofet," he pointed to the first guy in the back row and continued in order, "Zalman Gilboa, Avner Dror, me, Daniel Leon, Eldad Shoham, Saul, and Avner Gutman."

"Wait," I said as he was about to close the booklet, "Daniel from Cfar Shibolim?"

Daniel Leon was a childhood friend of my stepfather, Dubi. When we were little, Dubi used to tell us stories about their mischievous adventures together. Daniel committed suicide about a year after we moved to Cfar Shibolim. I never knew he had a connection to my father.

"Yes, may he rest in peace," said Yoav. "Did you know him?"

"Not really, but I remember when it happened, when he died. I was in sixth grade. They told us it was an accident. He had a son, a year younger than me, and they didn't want him to know his dad killed himself. I learned the truth years later."

Yoav nodded, then continued with his story. "Saul and I connected right away. Probably because we were both a year older than the others since we did a gap year. We also were the only ones with steady girlfriends. They weren't married yet, were they?"

"No, they got married a year later," I replied.

"I remember him as a bit disorganized with the gear and staff... and impulsive. Also, he was always loud with his opinions and complaints. We all had different personalities, but we came from a similar background, and at any rate, when you go through that kind of training together, you become close."

"What do you mean when you say he was impulsive?" I asked.

"For example, we used to get care packages from the kibbutz or parents, and Saul would always open them, even if they weren't for him, to see what's in it. I have a drawing..."

It's a funny one, this caricature. Dad, with the red hair and the mustache, is large in the middle, bent over a package. Black lines mark the trajectory of items such as cans, fruits, and snack bags pulled from the box and flying in the air, hitting the three soldiers standing around and knocking them down. The caption says, "A package arrived, and the Ginger "examines" it."

"We called him Ginger. I mean, he had red hair, right? Now, I don't know if gingers behave like gingers because they are expected to or because they really have a "short fuse" personality. But he was also very generous. When we went on patrols at night or early mornings, it was frigid in the open command car, so we had special jackets and blankest to wrap ourselves in. If someone was missing an item, Saul would always offer his if he didn't need it on that ride."

"What did you look for on those patrols?"

"Our job was to check the entire southern border for any sign of terrorists crossing from Egypt or Jordan. We had Bedouin trackers with us. They could identify any footprint or other signs of irregularity and follow them. We began every day at sunrise, and only after we checked the entire area we would stop and make a late breakfast. We had cooking equipment with us, and we would dig a hole in the ground and build a fire. We had a large pan and made a kind of scrambled eggs dish with all sorts of meat and whatever we got. Sometimes, we captured wild animals, like porcupines, and added the meat to the mix. We learned from the Bedouins to hunt and to eat with our hands. The rest of the day, we were free, and we often used the time to explore the area. You see things, plants, and animals you never see on the main roads. We had the privilege of the best all-terrain vehicles in the army and knew we could get assistance if the vehicles got stuck. Earlier, when you told me you studied veterinary medicine, I thought how fitting it was because of how your dad loved nature."

The house phone rang, and Yoav apologized – he must take the call. I used the break to watch some of the footage I'd recorded so far. It was weird how that person Yoav described was both familiar and not. It made me think of a documentary about Hurricane Katrina I watched a while back. In the film, the camera follows an older man who returns to his flooded home for the first time. The place is all brown and gray, buried under mud and mold. But as he walks through it, the owner begins to uncover familiar things. He wipes the dirt off a family photo to reveal the picture still intact; he picks up the colorful pieces of a favorite vase, thinking he may be able to repair it, and through his descriptions, one was almost able to see the place as it was before the disaster.

When we resumed, Yoav again began speaking without waiting for a question.

"Once, during our early days in the unit, I got into a jam with Saul. Every week we had a movie screened in the base's dining hall. One time, during movie night, Saul was on watch duty, meaning he was patrolling the base or manning the gate for a few hours. I guess he passed by the dining hall, and the movie grabbed his attention, so he stood there watching through the window. Now, you have to understand that the unit's atmosphere was relatively casual, unlike most army bases; I don't want you to think I'm some snitch, but I noticed him and jokingly pointed him out to the officer sitting next to me. I didn't do it to get him in trouble, just... I don't know what I was thinking, but the officer took it seriously. They were doing construction at the base at that time, and there were all kinds of building materials, so the officer told Saul to grab a window frame, just the frame without a screen or glass, and walk around with it until further notice. I don't remember how many days he was stuck with it. Of course, he got angry with me. Here, that's the drawing, which is how I remember that story."

He held up the next caricature. It's a simple one. Saul, in uniform and army boots, is standing alone, his head and left shoulder sticking through a rectangular window frame he carries like a messenger bag. A bubble over his head reads, "What did I do to deserve this?" While his right arm is motioning in an *I don't know* gesture.

"Even from this punishment, you can tell how unusual our unit was, and it was a good fit for us. We were lucky to find ourselves in such a guerrilla unit. Of course, there was a chain of command, and we respected it during operations, but we could also talk to the officers and even argue without getting in trouble. Once, we were driving back from the morning patrol and passed by watermelon fields. Our commander told us to go pick up some melons to bring back to the base, and Saul said no, we are not thieves, a farmer worked hard for those, and he won't touch them. And the officer respected it, even though Saul was sort of refusing an order."

Surprised, I felt pressure build behind my eyes and realized I'd been imagining that young guy, impulsive, messy, generous, honest. And I missed him so much.

Yoav, (luckily) oblivious to my brewing tears, continued.

"We weren't pacifists or anything, but we didn't care much about the army. We were brought up to serve the country and had every intention to do it properly, but we didn't have any aspirations for higher ranks and such. We both turned down officer training and other professional courses."

"Did officer training mean signing up for a longer army service?" I asked.

"Yes, officers had to serve an extra six months, and we both wanted to finish with the army so we could have a real home with our wives. I remember one time... it's a bit personal, but it was a long time ago," Yoav said timidly. "We had a party at the base, and both Alona and my wife, Aliza, came. After the party, Aliza and I wanted to be alone, so we walked to a classroom that was supposed to be empty. On the way, we ran into Alona and Saul heading in the same direction... Saul said, "You go ahead; we will figure out something else.""

"When were you discharged from the army?"

"I think in December 1955."

"65."

"Yes, yes, of course, 65. And you were born soon after, right?"

"Yes, April 66."

"I think it's fortunate he married and had two girls so early. If he waited, like today, nobody marries until they are 30, maybe he would have never had that chance."

I never thought about it this way, but Yoav was right. After Dad got sick and separated from my mom, it took many years before he again formed a long-lasting relationship with a woman.

"Did you keep in touch after the army?"

"For a while. Here, I should have a picture of you."

He grabbed the photo album and found three similar images. In the black and white photos, I'm about two years old, naked, in a small inflatable pool with three boys.

"Are those your children?"

"This one is," he pointed. "One of the other two is Roni's son. I don't remember who the third one is. Do you remember Roni and Dassi?"

"The names sound familiar," I said.

"They lived in the States for many years but are back in Israel now. Maybe you can talk to him. He is originally from Admat, so Alona can get you his number easily."

"Did you all serve together in reserve duty?"

"In the Six Days War, we were in the same battalion but probably not the same company. I don't remember seeing Saul there. I was also in Karameh but didn't see him there either. Only later I heard about what happened."

When I got back to my mom's house, she waited for me with lunch; an assortment of vegetarian dishes in small plastic containers she brought from the kibbutz dining room.

"How did it go?" she asked as soon as I walked in.

"Good, I think. He was very nice and eager to talk. He mentioned someone named Roni from Admat. He said maybe I should talk to him."

"Of course, Roni and Dassi. Yes, I heard they are back in Israel. Varda, you know, my childhood friend from Admat? She told me they made money from real estate transactions, then lost almost everything in the market collapse, so they came back. I can get you his number. I know who to ask."

"Yoav also mentioned Daniel Leon. I didn't know he was in Shaked with Dad. I always knew him as Dubi's childhood friend."

"Really? You didn't know? Well, I guess it's a little too late to talk to him."

We continued eating, each of us wrapped in her thoughts when Mom said, "You know, after Daniel died, I sat down with Ruth once, Ruth Cohen, she was Leon then, his wife...."

"I know who she is, Mom, and...?" I get impatient with my mom's convoluted sentences sometimes.

"It was a few months after it happened, after his suicide. I went one evening to see how she was doing, and she began talking about his depression. Apparently, he was depressed for a while but didn't want anybody to know. He was ashamed, afraid of the stigma of mental illness. And one of the things he said to her and repeated more than once was that his biggest fear was to end up like Saul."

Stigma

1980

I get up and pull my chair a few feet toward the building, chasing the late morning diminishing shade. It is summer vacation, and there is nothing to do. Around me, everything is dull, colorless, the dirty, off-white stucco building behind me, the patio stones bleached in the sun, the few trees in the distance covered in dust after months of no rain.

Like most days, my classmates and I got up at 4:30 am, had coffee in the dining room at 4:45, and were on the wagon heading for the melon fields at 5. At 9, we were done with the allotted daily work hours for 8th graders, had breakfast, and now the rest of the day stretches ahead, empty.

Inbal, next to me, makes a comment about an older girl passing on the sidewalk, something about the dress she wore on Friday night. The other girls chime in, but I have nothing to say. I honestly have no recollection of the garment.

Sitting on the stairs a few feet from us, the boys are arguing loudly. I can't tell if the foreign names they're throwing around refer to European soccer teams or music bands.

A man materializes in the distance, slowly dragging his tall, heavy frame up the road towards us. His oversized jean pants hang low on his hips, and a large, partly unbuttoned shirt drapes over them, lending the whole figure a shapeless form. He barely lifted his feet while walking; his head low, as if burdened down by the weight of existence. We all know him. It's Amir, a mentally ill kibbutz member. We are used to seeing him around, shuffling through the kibbutz aimlessly. We don't know much about him, only that he has always (or whatever fourteen-year-olds consider always) been like that. Sometimes he disappears for a while, presumably to some institution. Guy, our classmate, is his nephew, so whenever he sees someone from our grade, he always asks, in a somewhat feminine voice, "Where is Guy?"

He notices our group and heads over to where the boys are sitting. They greet him cheerfully as if addressing a child. He exchanges a few sentences with Guy, then says bye and see you later.

Before he walks on, he looks over at me and says, "Nitsani, (he always adds the I of endearment to everybody's name) How is your dad? Tell him I say hi."

And it's obvious to all present where he knows my dad from.

Setting the Record Straight

June 2015

Over the years, Dad was treated by many psychiatrists, but I could only recall a few, and most of them not favorably. Professor Yigal Ginath was the exception. So, when Dalia got in touch and managed to schedule a meeting with him, I was elated.

Both my parents always spoke highly of him as my dad's first psychiatrist, who was there in Karameh when Dad had his first episode and later diagnosed, as well as cared for him in the Talbiya hospital. Finally, we would get the full details of that fateful day in March of 68, of the catastrophic event that derailed Dad's life and upended our family's history.

Dalia and I arrived in the late morning at a two-story building in a quiet Jerusalem neighborhood. Ginath, a man in his late seventies with a mane of white hair and a matching mustache, opened the door to the apartment with a big smile and showed us to his home office. A large chestnut-brown desk, piled up with papers, stood in the middle of the room. Behind it, a bookcase bursting with books and publications leaned against one wall while simply framed diplomas and letters of appreciation crowded the rest of the space.

I secured the camera on a tripod, attached a neck microphone to one of Ginath's colorful suspenders, and when I was satisfied with the settings, I asked him to tell us about Dad and pressed *record*.

"In 68, I was a psychiatry resident, but I still served as a medical doctor on reserve duty, and that's where I was when the Karameh battle began. The operation's goal was to cross the Jordanian border to the city of Karameh, a known base for PLO terrorist attacks on Israel and capture the terrorist leader Yasser Arafat. The whole operation was a fiasco; a disaster of miscalculations."

As he said the last sentence, he shook his head. On his face was a mix of sadness and anger.

"The assumption was that the Jordanian army would not get involved," he elaborated, "but they did, with heavy artillery. We, at the medical clinic, were overwhelmed with casualties. Another medical unit suffered a direct missile hit to their field clinic, so we had to care for them and their soldiers on top of ours. It was a mess. A true nightmare."

"Do you remember what Dad was like when he was brought in?" I asked.

"No." Ginath seemed surprised at the question, almost outraged. "I didn't see him there. We were treating serious injuries and dying soldiers. Nobody had time for mental conditions. Only later did I hear about what happened."

Wait, what? I was confused. Of course, what he said made sense but was contrary to the story we knew. Our parents, or maybe just mom, right now I wasn't sure, always spoke about Ginath as the psychiatrist who happened to be in Karameh and was the first one to treat Dad over there.

"An infantry unit was guarding the bridge between Israel and Jordan overnight." Ginath continued, telling the events as he later heard of them. "One of the soldiers fell asleep on the road, and when our tanks crossed the bridge early in the morning, they ran him over. Saul and two other soldiers were ordered to collect the soldier's remains and bring them to the casualties' center. Saul refused; he said he couldn't deal with it, but he didn't have much choice and eventually, gave in and assisted. Then, on the way to the center, he started frolicking, singing, and acting in a way that was completely inappropriate to the situation. The other soldiers had to physically restrain him." From an early age, Dad told us about the tank accident. I think he even said it was someone he knew. But he never mentioned the incongruous behavior, and I never thought to ask how the crisis manifested in real-time. I wonder if he was embarrassed about it. It made me feel uncomfortable, imagining Dad clowning in song and dance in the middle of the carnage.

This kind of paradoxical behavior, cheerful in the face of tragedy and stress, is not unusual in extreme situations,» Ginath explained. «Soldiers from his unit later told me that he remained in an elated mood for the remainder of the reserve duty. Then back in the kibbutz, his mania accelerated. He had a wild love affair with a Dutch volunteer and stole kibbutz vehicles at night to go on high-speed rides. Eventually, his friends had to physically restrain him and take him to a psychiatric hospital."

"How come they brought him all the way to Jerusalem? Was it because they knew you?" Dalia asked.

"That might be part of it, but also because Talbiya was run by Kupat Holim (the national health insurance provider). Other hospitals at the time were either government-run or private. The privates were the worst."

"The worst?" I thought I misheard.

"Yes," he smiled, understanding my confusion. "Unlike the system in the U.S., the private hospitals here were horrible. Patient warehouses is the only way to describe them.

"Do you remember what he was like when you first saw him? What was the initial prognosis?"

"The thing with bipolar disorder, (in psychiatry, we no longer have diseases, just disorders) is that it can take many different forms. Some patients respond very well to treatment and lead relatively normal lives while on medications, and others cannot be adequately stabilized. They keep cycling up to manic states and down to depression, with some periods of normal function in between. I only took care of Saul initially, but from what I heard, his condition wasn't well controlled. As the person gets older, they often experience less manic states and more depression. If I'm not mistaken, Saul was mostly depressed in his later years, right?"

We both nodded.

"A person in a manic state is in an extremely cheerful mood, has unlimited energy, and might sleep just 1 or 2 hours a night. They don't understand why other people don't do the same, so they'll try to wake them up and get them to join in endless activities. They have heightened sexual drive, go on extreme shopping sprees, spend unusual amounts of money, and often fall into debt. They act carelessly and engage in risky behavior. Thinking becomes so fast that one thought is interrupted by the next, and the same is true for attention spans, which are short. They start ambitious projects and abandon them for the next project soon after. And the hardest part for the family is that the ill person can't stand resistance or attempts to restrict their behavior, never mind confronting them about it. If family or friends try to stop them from doing something rash, they can become aggressive, and because their self-sureness is so extreme, you can't talk sense into them. They enjoy a feeling of euphoria; of being omnipotent and will resist any attempt to stop them."

Everything Ginath was talking about was familiar, even obvious to us, yet there was something comforting in hearing it tallied that way. Especially the part about the impossible task of stopping a person who is in a state of mania. Time and again, I found myself cooperating, collaborating with Dad when he was "high" (the term we used in the family for the manic state). It was often just by pretending to believe the grand endeavor he was embarking on, the book he was writing, and the business he was building. Mostly I saw it as dishonest but harmless, like indulging the confusion of an Alzheimer's patient. But sometimes, it was more. Like the time I drove him, at his request, to the Tel-Aviv Boardwalk, which ended with an encounter with the police and a broken rib. On these occasions, I chided myself for taking the path of least resistance, for cowardly allowing my sick dad to head into danger. Ginath was articulating now what Dalia and I instinctively understood over the years. That there was no talking sense to a person in a state of mania and that confronting him will only alienate him but will not keep him safe.

"During these periods of mania, the depression awaits, just under the surface." Ginath continued, "And that's when they actually seek help. During the depression cycle, much of what they muse on is guilt about the destructive behavior they engaged in during mania."

"Could his bipolar disorder be a result of PTSD?" I asked, looking for an affirmation. "Honestly, no. It's not a typical PTSD response," he replied. "A typical PTSD presentation is flashbacks, nightmares, anxiety, and uncontrollable thoughts about the event. If he suffered PTSD on top of the bipolar disorder, it was completely masked by it. The traumatic event may have been a trigger, but there was probably some seed of bipolar prior to Karameh," he explained and shattered the myth we grew up with.

Post Traumatic Stress Disorder, formerly known as Shell Shock, carries its own stigma of cowardice, abandoning a post or mission, and putting fellow soldiers at risk while preserving the self. But for us, the Tank Story offered a neat explanation of Dad's condition. In it, Dad is a wounded soldier, a heroic status in the machoistic Israeli military worshiping society, whose injuries never healed.

The Tank Story was always an easy answer to the question, "Why is your dad like this?" And as a budding teenage pacifist, also an answer to why I was like that. Over the years, as we learned of other family members who experienced a transient period of depression and, on one occasion, what seemed like a singular manic episode, we came to suspect that genetics played a role in Dad's condition as well. But we always considered it secondary in significance to the traumatic event. What Ginath was saying now reversed that order.

"You know," he added after a pause, "I sometimes see cases, patients, older people who are only now, after decades of struggling, seeking help for their PTSD symptoms. Over the years, I came to suspect that a great number of Israeli men suffer from undiagnosed traumatic stress disorder."

While folding out the equipment, Ginath asked us about Dad's final years. How he was, how did he die.

"It was Avi from Ein Arava who called to tell me Saul died. Avi Rimon. He was in our army unit, and we stayed in touch over the years." Ginath said. "Did you talk to him? You should. He probably knows more details about what happened in Karameh."

Kibbutz

*"From each according to his ability,
to each according to his needs."*

(Karl Marx)

At the beginning of the 20th century, because of mounting antisemitism, many young European Jews joined the Zionist movement, which advocated for establishing a Jewish State in Palestine.

Those young idealists wished to leave what they considered "the old world" behind and embark on a radical new way of life in the Middle East. For practical and ideological reasons, many of the initial settlements in Palestine formed as a kibbutz, a democratic, socialist, agriculture-based way of life.

My grandparents were among those dreamers who immigrated to Israel in the 1930s, and so my father was born and raised in a kibbutz.

kibbutz members owned no private property but shared the kibbutz assets equally. Everybody worked at a job assigned to them based on their ability and the communal need, without monetary compensation.

In the early days of the kibbutz, men and women mainly worked in agriculture. They shared the manual labor, tended fertile vegetable gardens, sprawling cotton fields, fragrant citrus orchards, and livestock herds and flocks. Older school children worked one day a week and during vacations. Other kibbutz members worked in service jobs like cooking, cleaning, gardening, and childcare.

In time the kibbutz grew from a small settlement to an organized community with hundreds of members.

Each family was allotted a one-bedroom apartment called "a room." It had a small kitchenette, a living room, and one bedroom. A typical kibbutz residential neighborhood had a narrow central road meant for walking or bicycle riding, not cars. On both sides stood one-story structures, each with 4 identical front porches. The narrow lane that led to each entryway was surrounded by a minuscule garden with potted flowers, mint plants, and a bicycle rack. Each row of houses stood separated from the next by a grass lawn, usually strewn with weeds and sprinkled with thorny burrs.

At the heart of the kibbutz was the imposing square building of the Dining Hall. It served 3 buffet-style meals a day and was also used for weekly members' meetings, cultural events, and holiday celebrations. Mealtimes were much more than just food consumption. They were also the occasion for getting together, people watching, scrutiny and gossip.

A small store sold personal commodities, but instead of paying with cash, members charged their purchases to an allocated personal budget. Basic needs items like soaps or toilet paper were available in bulk for free.

The kibbutz owned several cars, and members could reserve them as needed. This fact is especially pertinent to my story since many of my father's escapades started with "borrowing" one of these vehicles.

One of the most talked-about establishments of the kibbutz was the Children's House. Children in the kibbutz did not live with their parents. Each age group, from weeks-old babies to high school seniors, had its own building. The children slept, ate, and spent the day in the Children's House, aided by caretakers and teachers.

Every day, around 4 p.m., a parent came to the Children's

House and took their baby or toddler home for the afternoon. Older children walked to the "room" by themselves. At 8 p.m., we all returned to the Children's House for the night. After a kiss goodnight, maybe a lullaby or a bedtime story, the parents left, and the caretaker or teacher stayed to make sure everybody fell asleep. There were no adults in the Children's House overnight. Every Children's House had an intercom that was connected to a unit monitored by night watchers. If a child cried, they would hear it and come over.

My mother grew up in a "moshav," or communal village, a watered-down version of the kibbutz or a hybrid between a kibbutz and a village. Financially, the moshav resembled a kibbutz; members worked at assigned jobs and shared the profits equally. The difference was in family life. Families ran a private household, mothers cooked and served meals, children slept at home. My maternal grandparents, of German descent, were strict and proper. Table manners, polite language, and overall appearances were important to them and enforced on their children. Mom, who preferred to see herself as a carefree "Sabra," (the term for an Israeli-born, rough and tough, named after the Sabras – a prickly pear cactus fruit) wished to live in a kibbutz, where children had more freedom and table manners were unheard of.

So, at the end of the 1967 school year, we moved to live on kibbutz Ein Arava where Dad grew up.

Mom was designated as a home-room teacher for the kibbutz's third grade, Dad joined the crew of the vegetable farm, a job he had done very well throughout his high-school years, and I was placed in my first Children's House with three other toddlers.

The babies and toddlers in the kibbutz were divided into groups of four, nicknamed "Foursome." Each group was housed in a small unit, a "Toddler's House" specially designed and built for that purpose. It was a white-washed cubical one-story build-ing with a small, fenced yard. Inside the fence was a sandbox, dotted with discarded household items for toys, a hand-built swing, sometimes an old piece of agricultural machinery for the children to climb on. Walking into the building for the first time, one felt like Snow-White in the dwarfs' house. Everything was child-size, from the toddler-height dining table and matching chairs, the four small beds together in one bedroom, the mini toilet bowl, and low hanging sinks in the bathroom.

I was too young to remember the move to the kibbutz, but my mom tells me that after a short adjustment period, I quickly got used to living in the Children's House, spending most of the day with a caretaker and the other 3 children. I probably felt closer to them than my baby sister, whom I saw only for a few hours every day and, as babies go, wasn't much fun to play with anyway.

I do have one memory from the "Toddler's House." I was probably two and a half or three years old. One evening after the parents put us to bed and left, I lay in my bed and could not fall asleep. I was bored, then I had an idea. I thought it could be fun to flood the "house." I can't say where I got the inspiration from, but I probably saw an adult overflow the sink by mistake and imagined the possibilities. I tiptoed out of bed, quietly woke up the other children, and showed them what I had in mind. We put a plug in the two sinks in the bathroom, opened the faucets all the way, then stood there, bouncing from foot to foot and giggling with anticipation as the water slowly rose in the basins and trickled down the sides. A puddle spread on the tile floor, then sent fingers of liquid in all directions. I moved aside when a small stream approached my feet, but Daniel hollered and flopped down smack in the middle of the largest puddle, and we all joined him, laughing and splashing in our self-made lake.

I had no recollection of how it ended, who discovered our mischief, and how they reacted, but years later, during one of his depression-induced self-loathing episodes, my dad suddenly asked, "Do you remember that time I spanked you?"

I was surprised. As far as I could remember, my dad never laid a hand on me.

"That time you flooded the Toddler's House?" He continued.

As it turned out, my parents were the first ones to walk in on the "flood." They were returning home from the weekly movie screening at the Dining Hall and decided to stop by the Children's House to take a peek at their Sleeping Beauty, who turned out to be playing Little Mermaid instead. My dad, in a moment of outrage, slapped me on my behind. It left a permanent mark. Not on me, but in his mind.

Spend Some Time

June 2015

Two days after my interview with Yoav, my mom called.

"I spoke to Roni Shofet," she said,

I was surprised. I thought she would get me his number and let me call.

"Well, I got his number from Varda, and I thought it could be interesting, an excuse to talk to him. I haven't spoken to him in years."

"And..?"

"He would be happy to talk to you. He lives in a moshav not far from the airport now. I told him you're in Tel-Aviv tonight, and he said he is free in the morning if you are. What time is the cemetery tomorrow?"

I made a quick calculation in my head. The headstone unveiling was planned for 3 p.m.; I needed to head North around 1. I meant to spend a quiet morning with my younger sister Efrat, but I could see Roni instead.

I followed the directions of the GPS to the address he gave me and arrived at a white, single-family house. A short guy with a shaved head stepped out of a side door and signaled for me to park on the side.

"Nitsan? Hi, I'm Roni," he said in a deep voice and offered his hand.

I followed him into a cramped kitchenette. He explained that he and his wife had lived in Arizona until recently but encountered some financial misfortune and, as a result, returned to Israel. They were now staying at a friend's "in-law" unit until they could figure out a permanent living arrangement.

He asked me about my children, and I showed him photos on my phone.

"He looks a lot like Saul," he said about Ben, my older son. "Not just the red hair, but the eyes and eyebrows."

I set up for the interview at a shady spot in the backyard. An airplane took off overhead, and I waited for it to pass. Roni smiled apologetically.

"You know, after decades as a pilot, I don't hear them anymore, but that's how it is so close to the airport. There's a takeoff or landing every few minutes. Nothing you can do about it."

I hoped the neck microphone would pick up his voice over the noise.

"So how should we do this? Do you want to ask questions, or should I just tell?"

I asked him to start and told him I'd ask questions as we go alone.

"OK, so I'll tell you about our first meeting," he said and went on to talk about his high-school exams prior to his draft date. He finally circled back to my dad.

"We were together in basic training, in the same tent, and then we went together to Shaked. Saul, he was different. In my opinion, he was a genius or close to it. He had a phenomenal memory, and as a result, he argued about everything. I can't recall him ever admitting he was wrong. He was into classical music, and wow, when it came to music, he could argue... I remember one time he announced there's no difference between the music of Bach and Handel. I said that, of course, they are different, and he said that if he played a piece for me, I wouldn't be able to tell which was which. We argued for hours, but to be truthful, he was right. It's very hard to tell them apart."

It was the second time this week I was told my dad was a genius. Coming from a guy as self-confident as Roni, an air-force pilot (Air Force entry exams are considered the hardest to pass in the Israeli army and pilots the cockiest), it was a significant accolade. All this made me sad because I never thought of my dad as an exceptionally smart person. Did the illness, or maybe treatments, erode his mental capacity, or was it just me, that couldn't see beyond his lack of formal education? My husband always said Dad was smart, and I would argue, saying he had a great memory, but that doesn't equate to superior intelligence. I remember deep philosophical discussions with my grandfather, Ezra, but not Dad. When I was younger, I mostly remember talking about day-to-day things, school, friends, events on the news. Sometimes we exchanged book recommendations. He loved Paul Auster and Lawrence Sanders. Later, when his deteriorating eyesight made it hard for him to read, and movie cable channels became available in Israel, he watched a lot of movies, and we talked about those.

Maybe he didn't think I was a worthy candidate for deeper discussions? Or perhaps we just didn't share subjects of interest?

"We also argued about other things, like ideology," continued Roni, "He was a true socialist, practically "Red" in his opinions. I was somewhat socialist back then, but over the years, I moved right." Roni rambled on about American politics, and I just nodded. I identify as socialist and consistently voted way left. It was good to hear that Dad shared the same views, at least in his youth. In later years, all I knew was that he consistently voted for the Israeli party that advocated for human rights, but he said it was because they helped the mentally ill. I think at some point, he got disillusioned with the kibbutz, and it affected his feelings toward socialism in general.

"I remember one argument on whether you can overturn a command car." Roni said, smiling at the memory, "I studied physics for the national exams, and I said that based on the laws of physics and centrifugal forces, it must be possible under certain conditions. Saul just said, "I tried. It's impossible.""

"Did you keep in touch after the army?"

"Of course. After his discharge, he and Alona went to live in Admat, and I'm also from Admat, so we were there together for a while. I was a track athlete; I competed nationally but didn't get any support from the moshav. They didn't allow me to take off work for competitions, and Saul would tell me, "Just go, what's the worst they can do to you?" He was like that. During that time, he worked in the fields on a tractor. It's very repetitive work, plowing back and forth; so he would bring headphones and a transistor radio and listen to music. In the moshav, that was unheard of. They said he had to be able to hear the tractor or whatever. Obviously, it was nonsense. I mean, when I fly a plane, do I listen to the engine? But the older members got very upset about it, especially since he was an outsider, and even though he pretended not to care, I think he did."

My grandmother on my mom's side, who I loved dearly, but was not the most tactful person, told me once she never particularly cared for my dad. At the time, I took offense and didn't ask her why. Hearing that story and being familiar with the moshav's attitude (very similar to that of the kibbutz), I now see how my dad's unorthodox behavior would embarrass her. Those groups revered, above all, the erasure of the self for the good of the community. They also looked down on outsiders and newcomers. It was unusual, almost unfathomable, for a kibbutz-raised person to defy age-old conventions, especially for his own enjoyment.

"Do you think any of this could be, in hindsight, interpreted as mental instability?" I asked. It's a question I was curious about.

"No, no, he was nonconformist, different, but what happened later was a shock. To everyone. Totally unexpected. By then I was studying in Jerusalem, and Alona called us. We went to visit Saul at the Talbiya Hospital, Avner also came with us, he too, had been injured. It was obvious Saul wasn't okay. He talked nonstop about everything...filtering nothing; it was hard to see him like that. Especially the way he talked to Alona."

"Like what?"

"He was very rude, offensive. But I was optimistic, or naive; I was 22, I thought, "Okay, he's going to get some medical and psychological help, and he'd be fine. He'll go back to a normal life." When Avner told his dad about the situation, he said the medical field doesn't know how to cure those kinds of things, and if you're like that, that's it; you never come back. I argued and said that couldn't be true. I didn't want to believe it, but I suppose he was right," Roni shook his head, "It was just another disaster on a long list of injuries and losses we suffered from and after the Six Day War."

"What about later? Did you keep in touch after those first hospitalizations?"

"Yes, yes, we were in touch for years. I even visited him once in Ein Arava. But when I started pilot training, we sort of drifted apart, you know, we had less in common."

Not the answer I was hoping for. I was trying to get at something. A memory I had.

"Do you remember a time he visited you with me?"

"Yes. We lived in Aseret; I'd just finished pilot's training."

"What year was it?"

"I wanna say the end of 1970 or beginning of 71. How old were you? Three?"

"Four or five"

"What he did, I think... He stole a bus or a truck, I'm not sure, and drove around with you to visit friends."

"How did he behave?"

"Unstable, talked a lot. He arrived with you, told me how he got the truck, talked nonstop for a long time. That's mostly what I remember."

"Did you know he took me without permission?"

"Yes. He said that… He said that…." Roni nodded, staring ahead, peering at a distant memory. "He said, 'I took her because I wanted to spend time with her.' How do you respond to that?"

"Do you remember how long he stayed? Did we sleep over?"

"You know, I don't remember. Maybe Dassi would. I don't think so. We had a tiny house and two babies, we didn't have space, but I also don't think he wanted to. He was on the move."

I was trying to imagine the situation from Roni's point of view. What would I do in his place? Would I try to stall Saul and call the worried mother? Would I ask him to stay, so at least I knew they were in a safe environment? Or maybe I'd be too afraid of a confrontation? Worried about my own family? Prefer that he leaves?

"We also visited him once in Nuweiba," Roni continued, "A few years later, when I was already a pilot."

Nuweiba is a coastal town in the eastern part of the Sinai Peninsula. Known for its carefree atmosphere and spectacular reefs, it is a popular getaway spot for young Israelis and European tourists. I remembered Dad vaguely talking about his love for the area and spending time there, but I couldn't recall any details.

"Nuweiba? Do you remember when?"

"It was after 73, so 74 or 75. Something like that."

"What do you remember?"

"Again, he talked and talked…about anything and everything, a lot about sex… Do you want more coffee? Water? You sure?"

"Thanks, I'm Okay. Tell me more about that time in Nuweiba. You're our first eyewitness from there. It might be the time he ran away from the Mazra hospital."

"Could be. Look, I don't know much… I asked about him, he was using another name, I don't remember what it was, and people warned us, asking who he was to us and be careful and stuff like that. He must have been acting weird. He had a girlfriend, a Danish tourist, I think."

"Where did he live?"

"He was in a tent, on a mattress; I don't know what he lived off, what he ate, I guess whatever he could find."

"Interesting. Do you think you have photos from there?"

Yoav said Roni was the photographer of the group.

"I can check, but unfortunately, a big chunk of our family's history made it into the stomachs of mice and now probably in their offspring's DNA. When you start working on the film, remind me, and I'll look again."

While I packed up, he asked me who else I was planning to interview and mentioned a couple of other guys from Shaked. He also mentioned a woman named Talia. He said she was also from Admat and came with him to visit the mental hospital in Jerusalem. She may remember more of that time.

The name Talia sounded familiar. Someone my dad kept in touch with over the years and mentioned occasionally. I wondered if it was the same person. If she was from Admat, Mom would know how to find her.

I had a two-hour drive ahead of me, and as I maneuvered the Friday afternoon traffic, I thought about the interview. Although Roni talked about himself more than Dad, I still learned a few things. It was as if the cardboard cutout of my dad as a young man was slowly filling up into a three-dimensional shape. And I could envision that brilliant, impulsive, red-headed guy, his large hand completely engulfing mine, shrugging his shoulders in defiance, saying, "I just wanted to spend some time with
her."

Medical Records

2012-2013

DO YOU HAVE TIME TO TALK? I'VE GOT SOMETHING INTERESTING TO TELL YOU. Read the text from my sister.

When I call, she gets straight to the point: "Do you remember Eliyahu Goldman from Assif?".

"Goldman? Yes, I think so. The artist? Wasn't his daughter in my grade? What was her name?" I recalled a small man, quiet.

"You remember he wasn't completely Okay?"

I did. He was a bit odd, but as a child, I didn't know or try to give it a label.

"Turns out, he suffered PTSD during the Yom Kippur War, and many years later, he sued the ministry of defense and was recognized as a wounded veteran."

Seriously? Recently? The implications were enormous. A disabled veteran in Israel gets a significantly higher monthly payment than anybody on a general disability. They also get a bigger allowance for home care, transportation, and other benefits.

We often wondered why the kibbutz never applied for such recognition on behalf of our father. I do recall Dad talking about it periodically, saying he would sue the defense ministry. But he never went through with it.

"You think we should try?" I asked. "Would you talk to the lawyer? "

"I'll call him. We should at least understand what the chances are and the cost."

A few days later, she spoke to the lawyer. He told her that before anything could be done, she must get medical records of Dad's first treatments to prove the illness and how it began. She called Prof. Ginath, hoping he would help gather medical records and write a letter on his behalf. He agreed to write a letter describing the first incident and request whatever paperwork survived after 44 years. In December, when I came with my family to visit Israel and celebrate my son's Bar-Mitzvah, we were still waiting on the paperwork.

One afternoon, sitting with Dalia in my mom's kitchen, the subject came up. Mom, who was nearby, heard us and asked what we were talking about. Dalia gave her a brief update.

"You got in touch with Ginath? That's incredible." Mom said. She dried her hands on the kitchen towel and came to sit with us. "Did he tell you what he was going to write?"

"No," Dalia explained, "He said he would need to request the medical files to refresh his memory. It might take a while. Because it happened so long ago, they no longer keep the records in the hospital and getting them from the archives takes time. But he remembered Dad well. He said he kept in touch with some army friends from Ein Arava and occasionally asked about him."

Mom nodded but didn't reply, just straightened the small pile of coasters on the table.

"How come the kibbutz never applied for him back then?" I asked.

"Well," she inhaled deeply, "I think there were a few reasons."

"Like?"

"First of all, PTSD, or Shell-shock as we called it then, wasn't as well known. I don't know if anybody in those years was recognized as a wounded soldier for it."

I later looked it up. When Dad got injured in 1968, PTSD was not an official diagnosis. It was first added to the DSM (Diagnostic and Statistical Manual of Mental Disorders- The official medical authority on mental conditions) in 1980. The Vietnam war and its effect on soldiers contributed significantly to the understanding of the condition, particularly its chronic nature and crushing consequences.

"But..." Mom stopped, and I sensed some discomfort.

"But what?" I asked.

"Well, I don't want you to get me wrong. He suffered so much and deserves any help he can get."

After a few more disclaimers and apologies, she finally got to the point.

"Karameh was the first hospitalization, but it didn't start there."

"Really?" I said. "Dad always said it began with that tank accident. You never said it wasn't true."

"Well, yes and no." She paused again, and seemed to examine an unseen dirt fleck on her bare fingernail. "He started acting weird a couple of weeks before going to Karameh. He worked at the vegetable farm in Ein Arava and was responsible for a section, a certain produce, I don't remember what it was, but he took it very seriously. He went to check on it after hours and even in the middle of the night. He was not sleeping well because he was worried about the crop. Or at least that's how he explained it back then."

Dalia and I nod in unison, recognizing the early symptoms of mania. For us, it's like hearing one's native language, immediately clear, intimately familiar.

"At some point, I began to think maybe there was something excessive about his behavior," Mom continued, "I mean, it was vegetables, not babies. What could possibly happen to them in the middle of the night?" She paused on the rhetorical question, and we smiled.

"Did you talk to anybody about it?" Dalia asked.

"I spoke to Grandma Deborah. She also noticed it. He was

overactive, talked a lot," Mom hesitated, searching for the exact word, "restless; I think that's what we called it, restless. I think... no, I know, I remember, she did talk to the kibbutz's doctor, but I don't remember if we had a chance to do anything before he went to Karameh."

"I remember something about another woman, a volunteer. Was that also then?" I asked.

"Yes, yes, it was. You have a good memory. She was a young volunteer from Scandinavia, or maybe the Netherlands? Tall, pretty. One day he came and said he had fallen in love with her, and he was planning to go with her to her country. I told him that if this was how he felt, I was not going to try and stop him. "

"You tell it so casually, weren't you upset?" Dalia asked.

"I was surprised, of course, but I didn't take it too seriously. I didn't think he was actually going to do anything about it. Later, he told me he was insulted by the fact that I didn't try to change his mind or ask him to stay."

"So what happened with that?" I asked.

"Nothing. A day or two after, he already went to Karameh. "

"You didn't think maybe he shouldn't go on reserve duty in that state?"

"Nobody knew it would turn into a military operation. We thought it was just routine training."

"Handling weapons and stuff?"

Mom looks at me for a long second, then shrugs. "I don't know. I didn't think about it that way. Suicide wasn't a concern at all. The opposite, he was so happy."

"But some kind of an accident?" I insisted. Not that it mattered, it was ancient history now. I was just trying to understand their state of mind at the time. Mom shrugged again and shook her head.

"Do you remember who told you about what happened? What did they say?"

I'm curious to know how the event was described. Did they call it mental illness right away?

"I don't remember getting a phone call or a message. I don't know who told me. Maybe they called someone else? His parents? The kibbutz? We knew by then that his army unit had taken part in the Karameh military operation and there were many casualties. We were told that he had a collapse or breakdown during the fighting and the army doctor, Doctor Ginath, who was also a psychiatrist, had him hospitalized in a psych ward."

We were interrupted by our kids who rushed in, excited and sweaty, competing over who would tell us first about the stray kitten they almost caught in the playground. We dispersed to tend to five pairs of muddy hands and one scraped knee.

A few weeks later, on a Thursday morning, a one-line e-mail pinged in my inbox,

"Attached for your review... Dal."

The attachment was labeled "Dad material Prof Ginath."

I clicked on it to reveal four poorly scanned pages of medical records, tightly covered with rows of the unevenly shaded letters typed on a bygone machine.

Original medical forms of my dad.

I quickly saved the photoshop file I was working on and began to read:

First hospitalization

Intake: 5/9/1968, Discharge: 7/14/1968

Wait, what? May? I thought Karameh was in March. I'm usually pretty good with dates (like Dad). I opened a new window and typed Battle of Karameh. The Wikipedia page read:

"The Battle of Karameh was a 15-hour military engagement between the Israeli army (IDF) and combined forces of the

Palestine Liberation Organization (PLO) and the Jordanian Armed Forces (JAF) in the Jordanian town of Karameh on 21 March 1968."

Confused, I read on.

Diagnosis: Dysthymic Disorder- Manic episode (presumably Bipolar Disorder)

What the heck is Dysthymic Disorder? A website called Betterhelp.com offered "dysthymia is also known as persistent depressive disorder." OK. Makes sense.

Genetics: The father suffered years ago from unspecified mental illness. 9 years old brother with severe retardation.

Funny. For years it's been clear to Dalia and me that the Bipolar gene came from Grandma Deborah. Her dad, according to her, had periods of "deep sadness." One of her nieces committed suicide, and Grandma herself had a manic episode once. Nobody talked about it, but Dalia was visiting when it happened, so we knew. But at the time this history was recorded, before the niece, before Grandma's event, Grandpa's eccentric personality made him the prime suspect. And maybe it was both of them?

Personal background: Oldest of 4 children. The father is somewhat eccentric, vegan. Normal pregnancy and birth. No abnormalities in childhood. Good student. Popular. Moody. As a teenager often stole kibbutz cars and went on joy rides. Did not finish high school.

In the army was in an elite unit. Met his wife during the service, and they married soon after.

In the Six Day War got into an argument with his commander and was demoted. Rumors of cowardice spread in the moshav, and he fought to clear his name.

I didn't know about The Six Day War thing. It was what, nine months before Karameh? I knew Dad fought there with the paratroopers' brigade who conquered Eastern Jerusalem and the Wailing Wall, but I never heard anything about the argument and demotion.

Was in reserve duty during the Karameh battle and experienced traumatic event- was ordered to collect the remains of a severely mangled body.

Wow, an official confirmation of the story I grew up with.

According to him, he experienced depression 4 times in the past. The first time was when he was 17, twice during army duty, and the last following the Six Day War.

I wonder if the depression at age seventeen is why he didn't finish high school. At any rate, not good news for our lawsuit.

Recent history: Soon after returning from reserve duty was with his wife on vacation in Jerusalem. On the last day started acting differently, told her things he had never told her before, and was overall restless. When they returned to the kibbutz, things got worse. He barely slept, claimed he did not need to sleep, took upon himself more responsibilities at work but was unorganized and inefficient. He initiated relationships with another woman, stole kibbutz cars for rides, told his pregnant wife he wanted a divorce. He refused medical treatment on the kibbutz and was hospitalized against his will.

I reread the paragraph. The description of Dad's behavior after Karameh matched almost perfectly Mom's memories. Only the timing was different. Significantly different. This explained the date of the hospitalization. Apparently, he was not hospitalized directly after Karameh but returned to the kibbutz first. It clarified a few more things. Like how come Mom and Deborah didn't try to stop him from going on reserve duty, or the fact she didn't remember who told her about Dad's collapse.

> <u>During hospitalization:</u> Has partial understanding of his condition. In the first days was loud, energetic, and very active. Follows the rules, never aggressive. His actions unorganized, goes from one thing to another. Shows some paranoia- often talks about kibbutz members who tied him down and forced him to get a tranquilizer injection. He threatened to sue them and even went to see a lawyer while on vacation.
>
> With the wife - was initially confrontational in his letters and wanted a divorce, but later repaired the relationship.
>
> At discharge showed understanding of his condition.

What did they mean by "understanding of his condition?" Did he understand that his entire life, from now on, will be that of a second-rate citizen? A kibbutz member of an inferior status? A father without legal custody? Did he grasp the enormity of the disease? I very much doubt it. In fact, I truly hope he did not. He was twenty-four years old. Just a kid. I want to believe that the realization came slowly, that he had time to adjust.

> <u>Physical exam:</u> Within normal limits.
> <u>Psychological evaluation:</u> The patient is very intelligent but unable to complete tasks due to occasional detachment from reality and psychotic thoughts.

This was followed by a long paragraph of psychological terms I couldn't make much sense of. Other than the final sentence:

No sign of mania or psychosis. Due to limited fortitude, psychological therapy is not recommended at this point.

Treatment: Chlorpromazine up to 600 mg a day.
Benadryl up to 150 mg a day.

Chlorpromazine is used in veterinary medicine as an antiemetic (treatment for vomiting) and a sedative. A search on Drugs.com revealed it is also "used to treat psychotic disorders such as schizophrenia or manic depression in adults."

As for Benadryl, its most common use is to treat allergies and as a sleep aid. I found one mention of using it to treat the side effects of certain medications. 150 mg is a very high dose. Tylenol PM, for comparison, contains only 25 mg of it.

Second hospitalization
Intake: 3/10/1969, Discharge: 6/12/69

Three whole months of hospitalization!

Diagnosis: Dysthymic Schizophrenia, Maniform wave, Paranoid thoughts.

If I understood correctly, in 1969, psychiatry considered Schizophrenia and Affective (mood) disorders as a spectrum or different manifestations of the same disease. Today they are viewed as separate entities.

<u>History:</u> Since his last hospitalization was mostly in low mood and reduced activity. Continued to work the whole time but without enthusiasm. He was given antidepressants but didn't take them consistently. He was transferred to a different reserve duty army unit and was called for service.

I'm surprised. I assumed he was taken off reserve duty after the Karameh events and hospitalization.

This may have prompted a rise in mood. When he went to the service, he was already in an elevated mood, over-active, talking nonstop, barely sleeping, annoying the other soldiers. He was sent for an evaluation but escaped his escort, drove away in an army vehicle to his kibbutz, on the way damaging the vehicle. He was brought to the hospital by kibbutz members against his will. Resisted entering the hospital.

What cowers behind those scrubbed words "against his will?" What violence? What humiliation? Scenes from "One Flew Over the Cuckoo's Nest" and "Girl Interrupted" come to mind; giant, uniformed, stone-faced orderlies dragging and restraining my young dad, tying him down. Now I'm furious.

<u>At intake:</u> Disheveled, angry, loud, cursing, and fighting with others. Orientation and memory intact. Insisted he was well, contested the hospitalization, showed no understanding of his condition. No hallucinations observed, but some paranoia was evident.

<u>During stay:</u> At the beginning remained active, slept very little, wrote angry letters to his wife, blaming her for all his troubles.

Mom never mentioned any of this. I don't know if she blocked those memories or just didn't want to talk about them.

After we raised his medication doses, he began to calm down. During the stay, he tried to get involved with a female patient. He talked about leaving the kibbutz, suing them for using force when taking him to the hospital. Gradually calmed down but showed little understanding of his condition. Began going on short vacations, and one of them refused to come back and was taken out of the patients' roster.

The chart for the third hospitalization is missing.

Fourth hospitalization.
Intake: 4/11/1971 Discharge: 1/6/72

Hospitalizations are getting longer.

<u>Diagnosis:</u> Schizoaffective Schizophrenia.

<u>History:</u> After escaping from the last hospitalization (8/1970) returned to his job as truck driver and was in a relationship with a woman until 1/71. Then entered a maniform psychotic state believing someone was trying to harm him by poisoning his food. Was taken to the Kfar Shaul mental hospital. Discharged on 3/1970 (in the original record. They probably meant 1971). Had relationships with a female patient he met during hospitalization. In the last few days became agitated and restless, spent money, and got into fights.

<u>Hospital stay:</u> At admission, he is alert and cooperative, the mood is slightly elevated, thoughts are rapid but rational. Unlike previous hospitalizations, he has a partial understanding of his condition this time.

He calmed down quickly and showed acceptance of his situation. Agreed to take medications. Later developed mild depression that lasted until his discharge. In meetings, he expressed despair and regret for ruining his family relations and friendships and hopelessness about his future. When he felt better, he found a job in a factory. After finding out about his hospitalization, the factory agreed to continue his employment but at a lower level. We arranged for him to register for an auto mechanics course. Discharged at the beginning of the course.

<u>Treatment:</u> Chlorpromazine up to 600 mg a day.
Haldol up to 15 mg a day and taper down gradually.
Lithium Carbonate 1.75 mg a day, stopped since the patient didn't take it consistently. At discharge was not on medications.

There was also a cover letter from Ginath. In it, he describes Dad's behavior after he was instructed to collect the remains:

"He initially refused to do it, then became paradoxically cheerful, began to sing and guffaw, and had to be forced to be quiet. The elevated mood persisted after he returned to the kibbutz...."

Ginath goes on to describe the medical treatment and concludes with,
"This phenomenon, of a manic episode following a traumatic event is known, although uncommon. I had no doubt then and still believe that the traumatic event described above caused the manic episode."

"Interesting," I replied to Dalia. "The letter is trying to be helpful, but the records not so much."

I also forwarded the paperwork to Mom. She read it and replied:

"I did not remember the vacation in Jerusalem. I also didn't remember he was hospitalized through the kibbutz. I thought the work in the vegetable farm, the events there, were before he went on reserve duty... I guess I was wrong. I must have told myself the other version so many times that now I remember it like that. What is clear is that what happened in Karameh is the same as we remembered, and Ginath says the traumatic event could have accelerated his deterioration, right?"

The lawyer said that based on those records, he wouldn't recommend going ahead with the lawsuit, and we let it go.

Three years later, when I interviewed Mom on camera, she confidently repeated the same order of events as she told us during our kitchen table conversation. As if she never saw the scans of the medical file.

In an article I read recently, a scientist suggested that every time we recall a memory, we alter it slightly, storing it again in a modified form. The changes could originate from discussing it with someone else and incorporating their view of the event into ours, from trying to reconcile confusing facts or, from bridging missing information. If, on first retelling, you might say, "I don't remember how I got there, I probably took a taxi," a while later, you might resolutely recall getting there by taxi.

Why are some memories altered? It could be entirely incidental. You totally forgot about that time you had a car from work. Or there might be a reason for it. A fact you prefer to eliminate.

We are all familiar with forgetting and accept that we don't have a perfect memory as a natural occurrence. We readily admit we don't remember our first-grade teacher or the name of someone we used to know well. But false or altered memories are much harder to recognize. To the person recalling, they seem as genuine as any other event.

My mom readily admitted she did not remember the type of produce Dad was in charge of, or the name of the Scandinavian woman. At the same time, she told us with confidence those events happened before Karameh and Dad was taken to the hospital directly from the battlefield.

I don't know how or why Mom's mind created the new order of events or what could have caused the alteration. Maybe some of the occurrences of those two months after Karameh, like the vacation in Jerusalem, or the subsequent severe mania that developed while the entire kibbutz watched on, were too traumatic and were erased from her memory as a protective mechanism. Maybe Dad wasn't the only one who developed a degree of PTSD that year.

Chained

July 2016

"**O**ver there," the nurse pointed to a short, stocky man, wearing a faded green t-shirt. "Micky, you have guests," she announced.

Every face in the room, or at least those who remembered to wear their hearing aids that morning turned toward us.

Micky waved and expertly maneuvered his wheelchair between residents and furniture.

"Let me guess," he said and contemplated for a second, "You're Dalia," he pointed at me.

"Nope." I shook my head.

"Okay, I tried," he shrugged and smiled mischievously.

We've been trying to find more people in the kibbutz who were close to Dad in the early years of his diagnosis. We spoke to a couple of his classmates, but none of them lived on the kibbutz during those years, and they only knew about Dad's condition from other people. Other kibbutz members who were involved were no longer alive. Then Mom mentioned Micky, a kibbutz member in his nineties who was purported to have a great memory and used to work with Dad at the vegetable farm. This was how Dalia and I found ourselves at the kibbutz's home for the elderly.

It was a clear, sunny morning, and Micky suggested conducting the interview outside. He led us to what he referred to as a patio but was more like an open corridor that ran along the length of the building. It wasn't an ideal location for filming, but after some consideration, I suggested that Micky sit with his back to some shrubbery, so at least we would have an unobtrusive, if not attractive, background.

I set up the camera and attached the microphone, and we began.

"When I came to Ein Arava, I was charged with building a vegetable garden. Not for profit but for local consumption," Micky opened, pulling himself up to sit tall in the wheelchair. "I had experience working at a vegetable farm in my previous kibbutz. I was never a big guy but I was very strong. I practiced Judo and could work harder than any of the big guys." In the energy of the old man in front of us, I could easily imagine that tireless young guy.

"Both Deborah and Ezra worked in the vegetable garden in the early years. Deborah was very quiet and industrious. Efficient and hard working. Ezra, he was a character. He had this dry sense of humor and an aura of someone who doesn't care what others think of him. He worked well with the kids, but whenever they asked him for the time, eager to go on break or finish the workday, he would pretend to check the watch he never wore and answer that it was exactly "a little before later.""

I completely forgot about that phrase Ezra used so often. Hearing it now conjured up Grandpa, short, stocky (my husband used to call him a Hobbit. Not to his face, of course) with his salt and pepper forelock that always looked like he missed his haircut appointment and a playful smile.

"Saul began to work in the garden when he was a teenager." Micky continued, "All kibbutz teens worked one day a week instead of going to school. I remember him as a handsome, brilliant guy, hard-working, energetic. He had a lot of knowledge, and he could even win arguments with me." He emphasized "even."

"After his army service, he came back to the kibbutz with

your mom. They made a beautiful couple. But then he went to Karameh and came back a different person; serious, preoccupied. He told me about the accident, a tank that ran over a guy's legs and took them both off."

I wondered if he mixed up Dad's story with another event or if it just morphed in his mind. I didn't see a point in correcting him, in telling him the tank drove over the entire soldier, not just the legs.

"We didn't know what PTSD was then, but it was obvious he suffered trauma. Sometimes he stopped in the middle of work and just stared. I would go to him and ask, "Is it Karameh?" And he would nod. Micky demonstrated my father's distant stare, followed by a slow nod.

"Afterwards he began taking kibbutz cars without permission; hot-wiring them and going on trips. First in the area, to the Gilboa mountain, then one day he took a European volunteer with him, a woman, and they drove all the way down to Eilat."

"Do you know if he had a romantic involvement with her?" I asked, unsure what the proper term might be for the supposed relations.

"I don't know." He shrugged. "One day, the kibbutz director asked me and another strong guy who also practiced Judo to come with him and help take Saul to the Rambam hospital. The director drove, and we sat in the back with Saul between us. When we stopped at a traffic light, he opened the car door and jumped out. I was fast, so I ran after him and was able to catch him and push him to the ground. The other guy brought cuffs and tied him down. He screamed, "Help, help, they are kidnapping me," and a small crowd gathered. But the director showed them a letter from the doctor, and they left us alone." So, Dad didn't make this story up; kibbutz members did forcefully tackle him and tied him down.

"We got to Rambam, and two large men came out and took

him. I'll never forget how he looked at me and said, "What are you doing? Why are you leaving me with those people?"

I was surprised. I expected Micky to talk about the vegetable farm. I thought maybe he knew more about the alleged romance between my dad and the Scandinavian volunteer. I had no notion that he was involved in the forceful transfer of dad to the asylum.

I searched his eyes for signs of regret or apology but saw none. Instead, there was resignation. People his age, especially in Israel, who left Europe during War World II and fought in several wars, have already seen, suffered, (maybe even actively participated in) a lot of misfortune and injustice.

"When I next saw him, he was a broken person, dead inside. He came back to work but with no enthusiasm. Going through the motions. Just once, he started talking. He told me that from Rambam, he was transferred to an asylum in Pardes Hannah, where he was tied down with chains. Some other patients hit him, and one even peed on him."

Ginath talked about those old mental hospitals. He called them "human warehouses," a place to stash the mentally ill away from society. I was aware of the practice of tying patients to beds for hours or days, but I never heard of a level of indifference and neglect that allowed some patients to torture others.

I should have been angry, but at whom? Micky who "followed orders" and assisted the kibbutz director? The director himself? The kibbutz doctor? I don't think any of them acted out of malice. Dad needed help, and they took him to a facility they believed was appropriate for his condition. If anyone was to blame, it was a society that for centuries considered the insane a nuisance or danger to be put away, banished outside the city walls, or behind barred windows. The notion that mental illness could be treated with medications and that the afflicted are not in control of their behavior, that they suffer and deserve compassion, was slowly gaining traction since the 1950's but was, by no means, an established fact by 1968. Even Dad's family probably didn't know how bad the Pardes Hannah place was, that there were other options, not great but better. Lucky for Dad, he was resourceful enough to run away repeatedly and was eventually transferred to Talbiya, under the care of Dr. Ginath.

"Later, he was on and off in the kibbutz," Micky continued, either unaware that this last account is new to us or realizing how upsetting it must be and scurrying to move on. "The vegetable farm was discontinued, closed down, and when he was on the kibbutz, he worked at the pickle factory. I would see him around, say hi. Most of the time, he was okay, but once in a while, like a gear wheel with 2 broken teeth, he would get out of alignment."

A nurse approached us and asked Micky if he was coming in for lunch. He looked at me, and I sensed that this toil up memory lane was enough effort for him for one day. We wrapped it up and said goodbye.

"That was a good interview, wasn't it?" Dalia said when we were back in the car, and I agreed. Although we didn't learn any astonishing new facts about Dad or that period in his life, it felt significant. As if the picture we had before was painted in broad strokes and simple outlines, and Micky's descriptions added color and details.

The Talk

1970

Two years after Saul's first breakdown, on a Saturday after-noon, Alona went to talk to his parents.

Their apartment was at the edge of the kibbutz, across the road from the barn and the cowsheds. The tiny bedroom was Ezra's. It had a single bed and a small desk, surrounded by book-shelves bursting with books that spilled to the floor, mixed in with various publications and letters. The living room had a bed, where Deborah slept, covered during the day with a fading quilt. Next to it stood a small wooden table and 2 armchairs. Against the opposite wall leaned a low bookshelf with children's books and a transistor radio tuned to the classical music station. Alona took a seat in the old armchair in the corner; Deborah and Ezra sat on chairs across from her.

Alona had a good relationship with Saul's family from the start. His father, Ezra, a short, stout man, was fascinating, bril-liant, and witty. He was an autodidact; he had very few years of formal education during his childhood in rural Poland, but was well-read in philosophy, sociology, and Jewish literature. He often loaned Alona books, and later they discussed them. It was an intellectual connection like she never had with her own par-ents, and she cherished it. On the kibbutz, Ezra was known as a difficult person. He had firm opinions on morality and was stern and authoritarian with his family. He was the one who outright refused to move Saul's brother to a home, even though the child was severely debilitated from birth, did not communicate, and needed constant care. With absolute devotion, Ezra cared for the boy and insisted the rest of the family participate as well.

Alona's relationship with Deborah was also excellent. A tall, energetic, no-nonsense industrious woman of Austrian descent, she was quick to smile although not inclined to talk much. They never had any heart-to-heart conversations, but Deborah often helped Alona with the girls and was always pleasant toward her.

Without too many preliminaries, Alona got to the point. She told them she wanted to "move out of the room." That was the kibbutz term for a couple's temporary separation. In practical terms, it meant she would go talk to the kibbutz's management board and ask for other accommodations, a room where she could live without Saul.

It's been a rough two years. In the beginning, Dr. Ginath said it might just be a one-time thing, a collapse triggered by a traumatic event, and that Saul is likely to recover. He said that sometimes another minor episode might follow but most likely that would be it. However, things did not get better. Saul kept cycling between mania, which the family called "high," and depression, or "low." The last time Alona visited Saul at the hospital, she had a long and sobering talk with Ginath, and he told her that the way things were developing, it was probably going to be a lifelong illness.

She loved Saul, she explained and felt sorry for his situation, but the day-to-day living with him was unbearable. She wasn't thinking of divorce or anything like that, but an immediate, temporary solution to the current circumstances.

As she continued to elaborate, Ezra got up from his chair. In his heavy gait, and without saying a word, he left the room. Assuming he went to the bathroom or to get a glass of water, Alona continued the conversation with Deborah, who seemed to understand her difficulty. If she had any resentment for her decision, she didn't show it. After a while, it became apparent that Ezra wasn't coming back. He left, and that was it. That was his way of showing his disappointment, anger and resentment, and that Alona's decision to separate from Saul was, in his eyes, unforgivable.

At the time, Alona was sure there would be a chance to talk about it later. That at some point, he would try to understand or at least be willing to hear her out. But it never happened. He never spoke to her again. For the rest of his life, he did not talk to her or mention her name, not even to his granddaughters. He acted like she did not exist.

Letters

August 2016

I looked around for a street number or a sign. The old gray warehouse with a loading ramp at the back could be it, but so could numerous other properties in this rundown commercial neighborhood in Southern Tel-Aviv. The area seemed fairly deserted at this early morning hour, so I braved illegal parking and stepped out. When I got closer to the building, I saw the little sign on the side door, "Davidson Camera Rental."

I'M HERE, I texted and went back to sit in the car. When no reply came, I began to worry. Did I get the day or the time wrong? I scrolled up and double-checked the date and time we agreed on. Did he oversleep?

COMING. My screen flashed to my relief.

A guy came out the side door, pulling a trolley in one hand, an elongated tripod bag slung over his shoulder.

"Sasha?" I asked. He looked different from his profile picture. A bit older, shorter, and the big curly hair was now trimmed down to a cropped cut.

"Nitsan? Hi, here, you can load these," he said and handed me the equipment. "I just need to go back for some ND filters. I thought they were included with the bundle," he raised his hand slightly in the direction of the trolley and turned to walk back.

I was relieved. Whenever I work with male photographers, I somewhat expect, yet dread, the condescending "Let me take that, it's heavy," or worse, "Be careful, they're fragile." Those are usually early symptoms that later, into the work, will fester into challenging my vision. I had very brief communications with Sasha before we began, primarily to schedule, talk pricing, and equipment needs, but my first impression was that I liked him.

A few months back, during my last visit to Israel, I met my cousin on my mom's side of the family, Arnon, an experienced TV documentary producer. I told him that I'd begun working on a film about my dad's illness, and he offered to look over the outline.

He found the accounts interesting and, after some discussion, suggested that the search for information could become part of the story. At first, I balked at the idea. Mainly because it would mean that I would be filmed conducting the interviews and I don't like seeing myself on camera. However, I realized it's a valid concept, and I should keep it as an option. When I initially embarked on this project, my intention was to tell Dad's story in a straightforward fashion, but after filming a number of interviews by myself, and seeing how one led to the next, how some information was complementary, or contradictory, I could visualize the search as part of the plot, a frame for the story. To that end, I decided that on some of the coming interviews, I would bring a camera person along. They would film the interview in a similar way to mine, but they would also film Dalia and I arriving, meeting, interacting with the subjects. I didn't know any cinematographers in Israel, so Arnon suggested Sasha.

Sasha returned with the missing filters and doublechecked to see that we got everything we needed, while I entered the GPS coordinates to the Jerusalem parking garage where we were going to pick up Dalia on the way.

The road from Jerusalem, at 2,500 feet above sea level, to kibbutz Ein Gedi, by the Dead Sea, 1,400 feet below sea level, descends steeply, winding between sandy, yellow, desert hills, sparsely punctuated by low, colorless plants.

Dalia and I used the time to update Sasha on the assignment.

"The woman we are going to meet, Talia, is an old friend of our dad who kept in touch throughout the years. They wrote to each other, and she kept the letters, which is the main reason we want to meet her, but we figured we should also do an interview if we are going all the way to Ein Gedi," I said.

"She sounded very nice on the phone," Dalia added. "I think she likes to talk."

"Other than the interview, what else do you want to film?" Sasha asked.

"We should definitely film her getting the letters out of the storage box, bag, or whatever she has them in. Opening some and maybe reading a passage," I said.

"How about walking through the kibbutz, knocking on her door and all that stuff?" Sasha suggested.

There are two kinds of documentaries when it comes to the filmmaker's participation. In the more traditional form, the director is not part of the story, just an observer. In recent years, a style embracing the active participation of the filmmaker in the film gained traction (think Michael Moore). These movies will usually open with the director explaining how and why they decided to make it, their personal connection to the story, and what they are trying to find out. In the first kind, the filmmaker is never heard or seen on screen. In the second, they will often narrate the movie in first-person voice and will usually be seen doing research (or, more likely, recreating for the camera a photogenic researching scene), knocking on doors, meeting the interviewees, and spending time with them.

We passed the sign "Sea Level" and continued our descent. As kids, we used to hold our breath and pretend to go underwater when we drove by it.

On our left, the view opened to reveal the sapphire oblong

of the Dead Sea, and on the other side of the Great Rift Valley, shrouded in haze, the golden mountains of the Jordanian Kingdom. Sasha picked up his camera to film the scenery through the car window.

We parked at the kibbutz parking lot, and Dalia called Talia to get instructions to her apartment. There are no streets on any kibbutz and no addresses. The only way to navigate the lattice of walkways is by old-fashioned directions, "follow the road as it curves to the left and turn right by the green waste receptacle."

We identified Talia's home by the lush vine covering the pergola at the front. We paused to decide on the best angle to film our entrance when a small woman, her graying hair in a messy ponytail, opened the door.

Dalia, who was closer, extended her hand in greeting, but Talia didn't seem to notice. She looked distraught, talking rapidly, flailing her hands in large gestures.

"I'm so sorry..." was all I could discern. Sasha put away the camera, and I approached, catching only fractions of words.

"Wait, what happened?" I asked, alarmed.

Talia paused and looked at Dalia, leaving her the task of delivering the news.

"She can't find the letters," Dalia started, and Talia, emboldened by my smile, lounged again into a convoluted explanation on how she was a hundred, no, a thousand percent sure the letters were in that particular box, where she also keeps this and that and...

The bottom line was that the promised letters were nowhere to be found. There was only one short postcard.

From the few letters I had from my dad, I knew he wrote skillfully, and his letters were often detailed and earnest. I had high expectations, and I was now fighting to keep my emotions in check, or at least from showing on my face.

We followed Talia into the apartment and accepted her

offer of cold water. Then Sasha, looking through the camera lens, directed us to sit on two adjacent couches. At first glance, I thought they were a set, but on further inspection, I realized they were of two different styles; both faded over time to a similar shade of gunmetal blue. The rest of the apartment was decorated in the same fashion. There was an accumulation of mismatched photos and drawings on the walls, books arranged on shelves, and the ones that didn't fit piled up on top of the others. A plethora of decorative figurines, rocks, vessels, and a few items I could only assume were mementos. Of what, I couldn't tell. When Talia said again that she is sure to find the letters at some point because she never throws away anything, I believed her.

"How did you meet Dad?" I asked when Sasha signaled the camera was running.

"I'm from Admat," she replied, "so I've known Alona since childhood. I remember she told me she met a guy, but when they got married and came to Admat, I was a student in Jerusalem, so I didn't meet him. Then once, when I was home for the weekend, she told me there was this fight or argument between the field workers. Saul, apparently, was listening to music with headphones on the tractor," here she made a hand motion of pulling headphones over her ears," and the director of the fieldwork, it was Yanka'le Levi, told him he can't do that, he must constantly be alert to what's going on around him."

Dalia and I nodded. We'd heard that story before.

"And I said to her that I think Saul was right, and they were just picking on him, and I guess she told him that I supported him. I'm not sure I exchanged a single word with him at that point. And then the whole thing with Karameh happened."

Talia made a large twirling hand gesture to punctuate, and Sasha interrupted and asked if she could possibly remove the assortment of bangles rattling on her wrist because they interfered with the recorded sound.

While removing the bracelets, she continued. "Roni, you know Roni Shofet?"

"Yes," I replied, "he was the one who recommended we talk to you."

"Yes...right...So he went to visit Saul in Talbiya, and Saul asked about me. Said he wanted to see me. I was surprised," she raised her eyebrows and widened her eyes. "But I agreed. Alona told me later that during that time, he avoided most people. He was ashamed of his condition and wanted only to meet people he thought would be sympathetic. And I guess because of what I said before....»

A hint of something hung in the air for a split second. An unspoken understanding that maybe he hoped for more than a friendship.

"I shared an apartment in Jerusalem with my sister and other students from our high school, and Roni brought Saul over. I mostly remember how he tried hard to show he hadn't lost his mental capacity. One of us had a map, and he showed us he could recite the names of all the rivers in the South in order. That's how he was in the beginning."

I found it interesting that he would equate mental ability and memory with sanity. But then again, what did a young person in the sixties know about mental illness, other than the distorted, sensationalized way it was portrayed in books or films?

"It was just in the beginning that he was like that." She repeated, "there was this thing also... Roni told me, that they walked down the street, and he said he could read people, that he could say who is married or single (wedding rings were not common in Israel back then). And then he would ask them if he was correct. And Roni told him, 'Crazy or not, but most people wouldn't walk up to a person on the street and ask them if they were right about them.' He really had a need to prove his place in society. Then he did Okay for a while, and his doctors decided he could go back into the army as a reservist. He didn't want to. They thought if he functioned okay there, it meant he was fine. And he didn't."

"Wait, what?" Dalia interrupted. "You think he went into the army again after Karameh? Are you positive? That doesn't make sense."

"One hundred percent positive," Talia replied. "He did well after the first hospitalization and the doctors decided he could go back into the service. He was scared and stopped taking his medications. Then something happened. I don't remember the details, but he ended up in Talbiya again."

"You know what," I said to Dalia, "I think she is right. I vaguely remember something about it from Ginath's records. He ended up taking an army Jeep and damaging it or something like that."

Although I heard about it before, I still found the decision infuriating. I would be naive to think that if he didn't go, he would have been okay forever, but still.

"I thought about it a lot," Talia continued, playing with the rings on her fingers, "the post-trauma he had, I think it's a normal reaction. If what happened wouldn't have affected him, that would be abnormal."

"And since then, you kept in touch?" Dalia asked.

"Yes. When he was allowed to leave the hospital, he visited our apartment, and we would all have dinner together and talk. Later I moved back to Admat, and he moved around a bit. He visited sometimes and wrote."

"What did you talk about?"

"I don't know. Different things. He loved hiking and nature and showing his knowledge. Music also, but I was not as familiar with what he was interested in. He talked about his family, his sister in medical school, and there was a brother who needed special care?"

"Yes," Dalia confirmed, "he had a young brother with severe mental disabilities."

"He asked about my studies. He was interested in literature and psychology. He was very smart, he read a lot. We didn't talk about the hospital or the treatments, what they did there...I didn't ask. He did tell me the medications made him seem normal to the outside world, but he felt like he was trapped. And sometimes, he couldn't take it anymore, so he stopped taking them. Then he felt good for a little while, but after, there was always a down."

I've heard people say that about psychiatric medications before, but not Dad. To me, he always said Lithium was a life-saver. Were those different medications, or did he just get used to the effect of Lithium over the years?

"He was very sincere in his letters. In the earlier years he wrote about your mom. He still loved her, but he wasn't angry with her for leaving him. He wrote that he doesn't think he can get cured. That even if he has a couple of good years, eventually, he will end up in those places again. But later, he did have long periods out of the hospital, right? When he had that girlfriend. He talked about her and her son."

"Yes," Dalia said, "he had some good years.... when?" She looked at me. Dates are my department.

"I think from around 1980 to when he lost his driver's license in 2009," I said.

We consider them "The Good Years" because he was rarely hospitalized. He lived on the kibbutz and worked as a forklift driver at the pickle factory. He was in a stable relationship with a divorcee who had a child from her previous marriage. Were those mostly good years for him? I don't know for sure. We generally remember the manic episodes because they were outrageous and disruptive. We date them, give them names, "Geneva," "Abarbanel, (A.K.A. Telephone Guy)," "That time with the gas." But what about the times he was depressed? I vaguely remember those periods, but I cannot begin to estimate their frequency or duration. They all blend into a generic picture of Dad not answering the phone or hanging up after a short exchange. Those were indistinct, unmemorable. Only after my dad's passing, did I begin to read more about depression, to become aware of the extreme anguish that comes with it.

"For how long did you keep in touch?" I asked.

"Pretty much until the end, although he didn't write much in the last few years. It was mostly short "Happy New Year" calls."

"He didn't see well. I doubt he was able to write," Dalia explained.

"Did he write more when he was manic?" I asked.

"Both. But the best letters were from the times when he wasn't manic. He wrote about being home, by himself, not seeing anybody other than his mom. Listening to music. I don't remember the details, but the feeling was that he was able to look at his situation with acceptance. Look, I've been by myself for eight years now. That's my reality. I can't say I'm happy, other than when I see my grandchild maybe, but it is what it is."

She talked a bit more. About herself, about other people she knew in similar situations.

Before we wrapped up, I asked her to read aloud the one postcard she found, and Sasha filmed her and then some close-ups of the card.

Talbiya 4/7/70

Talia,

Just as the swallow brings the spring, the spring brings me to Talbiya, and when I remember Talbiya I remember your visit here a year ago and I wish for more.

I know you no longer live in Jerusalem but if you can find the opportunity to visit me I would be grateful. It's just that I'm

bored here and in need of some intellectual stimulus, your area
of expertise.

Goodbye and so-long,

Saul.

At the door, when we were ready to leave, she stopped us and
said, "You know you were everything to him, right? After the
separation from your mom, it was just you. He was very proud
of you. When I find the letters, you'll see."

On the way back to Jerusalem, Sasha sat in the back and suggested we talk a bit about the visit. It would make for a good
transition in the film.

"She sounded so sure on the phone she had the letters, I never
thought to question her further," Dalia said.

"I don't regret meeting her," I replied. "Out of all the people
we talked to so far, she was the only one outside the family who
seemed to have had a real friendship with him for all those years."

I thought about it later. What was it about Talia that allowed
Dad to be open and at the same time intellectually engaged?

My impression of Talia was of a highly intelligent and curious person but also friendly and accessible, nonjudgmental.
Not a common combination. That must have played a role. And
maybe also the fact that there was some distance, that they
never got romantically involved, that she didn't live on the same
kibbutz, didn't witness any of his outbursts, wasn't part of what
he imagined or knew to be the ongoing conversation about him,
the social isolation and stigma.

Whatever enabled this friendship, I was thankful for it, grateful for her.

A few months ago, I got in touch with her again. She was happy
to hear from me, and no, she has not found the letters yet. But
she will. She is sure of it.

Stork

1970

"Shhh," my mom whispers and rests her hand gently on my shoulder to stop me. I freeze, but it's too late.

It's a Saturday afternoon. The only time Mom and I can spend a few hours together, just us. During the week, I'm at the Children's House, and she's at work. In the afternoons, we have to take care of my baby sister. But now Dalia is at the Toddler's House, and Mom and I are taking a walk to see the migratory birds by the fishponds.

A cacophony of ear-piercing shrieks and flapping wings ripple through the air as a large flock of storks takes off right in front of us. I watch in awe as they turn into a cloud of dark specks against the azure skies.

"Did we scare them?" I ask as they disappear beyond the peaks of Mount Gilboa.

Mom puts a finger to her lips to signal me to stay quiet.

That's when I notice the stork on the ground.

Mom pulls out a pair of binoculars from her backpack and examines the bird. "I think she's wounded," she says and hands me the heavy lenses so I can see for myself.

The stork is slouched on the ground, head low, and it's long red beak is buried in the dry grass.

"Can we help her?" I ask.

"I don't know. Let's see if we can get closer."

We slowly, quietly advance toward the bird. It tries to move but only maneuvers itself a few inches, then gives up.

"I think her wing is broken," Mom says, pointing to the weird position of the limb.

The stork seems resigned to our presence and no longer attempts to get away.

"Can we help her?" I ask again. Even as a child, I understand there's no way a wounded lonely stork can survive by itself.

"If I can pick her up, we can take her to Didi; he'll know what to do."

Didi, a biology teacher and researcher, was the kibbutz's authority on all wild living things. The rumor among the children was that if you took a shortcut through his garden and damaged the plants, he would chop your head off.

Mom hands me the small backpack and the binoculars and bends down next to the stork. She puts both hands under its belly and lifts it.

"Is she heavy?"

"Not really."

"She's pooping on you," I chuckle, but my warrior, saver of the animal kingdom Mom, holds firmly, ignoring the excrements on her sleeve.

We take a shortcut through the kibbutz lawns toward our room. We can't go to Didi just yet. It's afternoon rest time, and no animal emergency justifies interrupting another member's nap.

I rush ahead, opening the door for Mom and shooing away Tula, our cat.

Mom places the stork on the floor, and we sit next to her and watch.

"Can I give her food?" I ask.

"Sure, here," Mom says and reaches for the backpack. She pulls out an uneaten sandwich.

I take one slice of bread, scrape off the margarine and expertly tear little pieces into a plastic bowl, the way I've seen the older kids do at the Animal Corner, the kibbutz's petting zoo. I add water and place it in front of the bird. It ignores it at first but then tentatively dips its beak into the bowl and flips it up to swallow.

The nourishment must have given it some energy because suddenly, it makes a jumping motion and stands up.

I am startled and step back behind Mom, but the bird doesn't move further. "Here, let's make her a little home," Mom says and lifts the protective wire mesh that is usually meant to keep toddlers away from the oil heater. It's three by three-feet square, three-foot-tall, and placed around the bird creates a perfect open-top cage.

At 4 p.m., we go to pick up my sister, and on the way home, stop at Didi's. Later he comes and takes the stork to the Animal Corner. I don't remember what happened to it. I like to think it healed and joined a flock the next migration season.

Kidnapped

1995

I'm sitting with my mom in her small kitchen. It's Friday afternoon, the end of the semester in veterinary school, and I'm here to visit for the weekend. She just woke up from her afternoon nap, wearing a loose house dress with pink and purple flowers. Her hair, dyed black, is resting on her shoulders, framing a wrinkled face that is still beautiful, with high cheekbones and big eyes. Her skin that used to be freckled is now age-spotted. She is standing by the kitchen counter, her back to me, pouring boiling water over instant coffee powder in a vintage mug. I'm drinking an Americano I picked up on the way.

"Do you know who I ran into yesterday? Remember Gideon Cohen from Ein Arava?" she starts, referring to a person from our old kibbutz, a place we left when I was 7.

"The name sounds familiar. Who is he?" I feign interest.

She pulls out a chair and joins me at the dining table, or what my parents (that's how I refer to Mom and Dubi now) use as a table. It's a rectangular slab of white marble, straight and rough on one side and ornately cut and finished on the other three. It used to be the top of the antique dresser now standing in the living room. For legs, the table has the base of an old sewing machine, with the pedal tied with a piece of wire to stop kids (or anybody with bouncy feet) from rocking it. Together with a church bench and confession booth (fitted with shelves, it's great for toys storage), an assortment of rusting coal irons, menorahs, rags, and painted tiles, It's part of my parents' eclectic home decor. Not the well-curated designer style that usually goes by that name, but a mix of salvaged antiques and household items, often rescued from a garbage pile next to a renovated home or church, and ethnic pieces from bazaars and flea markets.

"He's a really nice guy. Helped me a lot during the early years of your dad's illness." Mom continues. "He was the person in charge of security in the kibbutz when dad kidnapped you the first time. I insisted they wouldn't call the police, and he agreed and...."

"Kidnapped me?" I interrupt her. What the hell is she talking about?

"Okay, kidnapped may be a strong word. Took you without permission."

I still don't have the slightest idea what she's referring to.

"MOM, WHAT ARE YOU TALKING ABOUT?" I ask again, real slow, separating the words.

"You don't remember anything? We never talked about it?" She seems genuinely surprised.

"No."

Mom shakes her head, bemused.

"You were probably about three and a half or four." She says, "I think your dad escaped from the hospital. He was smart and fearless and always found ways. He took a car. To him it wasn't stealing. He needed a car, so he took one. Once, he even got into a bus at the central bus station, drove off and picked up soldier hitchhikers on the way. Anyway, that time, he showed up at the Children's House, and before anybody realized what was going on, he took you with him."

"Seriously? Where did he take me?" I was incredulous. My mom never kept any information from me. How is it possible that it's the first time I'm hearing about this?

"Well, it actually happened twice. The first time I think he took you to Tel Aviv."

I'm racking my memory. "Could it be that he took me to the zoo? I have an odd memory of a trip to the Tel Aviv Zoo and him letting me ride a giant turtle."

Mom chuckles. "Could be. He was manic, of course, so he might have done something like that."

I'm trying to think what else I remember from that day at the zoo, but I'm drawing a blank.

"We didn't know where you were," she continues, tucking a strand of hair behind her ear. "He called from Tel Aviv to say you were with him and not to worry, but of course, we worried. He was often speeding when he was in mania. Also, I was afraid he'd get stopped by the police for a traffic violation or some other foolishness, and I didn't know how he would react. He was unpredictable and unlikely to cooperate."

She doesn't need to elaborate. I get the picture.

"We called around to his friends, people we thought he might go to. Some of them saw you, like Roni Shofet and Ahuva Davidi. He knew we would be looking for you, so he didn't stay anywhere for too long."

I don't know who those people are, but I don't want to interrupt her.

"Then somehow, we found out he made an appointment with a lawyer for the next day. Maybe he mentioned it when he called, I'm not sure. He said he was going to sue the kibbutz or something. So, we went there to wait for him. Thinking about it now, it was quite funny." Mom smiles. "A few kibbutz members stood on street corners all around the block, hiding their faces behind newspapers with holes so he wouldn't see them, and waited. The lawyer's secretary was going to offer to play with you while they were meeting and then take you out and hand you to the waiting people." The image in my head is something from the "Emil and the Detectives" children's book, or maybe a Charlie Chaplin movie.

"Did it work? I can't believe I don't remember anything about it."

"No, we hung around for a long time, but he never showed up."

"So, how did you find me, or did he bring me back?"

"He didn't bring you back, but in the evening, we got a call from Grandma Anna, (my late great grandmother). "He arrived with you and asked to sleep over. He probably knew she would call us. He went out to the movies, and someone drove me to Jerusalem to pick you up."

I do have a vague memory of sleeping at Anna's. Could it be then?

"Do you know where we slept the first night?"

"Yes, He told me later you slept in the car because he didn't want people to come and take you."

Mom went to get dressed for dinner in the Dining Room, and I stayed at the table, trying to wrap my mind around that out-rageous story. My dad practically kidnapped me twice, and I barely remembered a thing. How is it possible?

It was the time before Google and smartphones. I didn't have easy access to scientific information about memory, just a bunch of theories. But later, I was able to read about it more. Research shows that the formation of autobiographical memory, mean-ing the memory of events (as opposed to the retention of facts), typically follows a few steps.

At first, the brain creates short-term impressions. These are non-distinct events we retain for a duration and gradually erase. In time, mundane activities are lost, and only certain occur-rences are committed to long-term memory. Those are usually unexpected, traumatic, or otherwise surprising events.

In children, memories and their significance are often medi-ated and shaped by adults' responses. If, for example, a child was involved in a near-miss accident and was unharmed, she might not perceive it as a notable event and might not remember it at all. But if for the exact same incident, an adult would react hysterically, the child is more likely to remember it as extraordinary and even traumatic.

Mom, consciously or not, tried to shield me. Not only from my dad's unpredictable behavior while he was manic, but from any fear of him. She did worry about my physical safety, but she also understood that my emotional well-being and relationship with my dad were at least as important. She was so adamant about protecting me, it took her twenty-five years to talk about what happened.

As a result, for me, the most memorable part of those two days was riding the tortoise, and I retained a fairly clear memory of it, although, for years, I doubted it actually happened. Only when I was able to find photos of the old Tel Aviv Zoo, and the tortoise enclosure was precisely as I recalled it, I realized it was real.

E-mail, Mother's Day

5/13/2018

Hi Mom,

It's Mother's Day here, and maybe it's a complete coincidence, but I woke up understanding that I need to tell you something. I don't know if I can articulate it well over the phone, so I decided to write.

I want to thank you for making sure that Dalia and I would have a close relationship with Dad; that we won't be afraid of him and will always respect him.

Even as a child or teen, I understood it was due to your efforts that we accepted Dad as he was, with the illness and unusual behavior, as someone who deserves compassion, not anger, shame, or blame. But only recently, I understand how hard it must have been for you, especially regarding Dad's irresponsible and dangerous behavior when he was manic. I don't know how much of it was a conscious decision and what part was because you pitied him or had other reasons, but it doesn't matter.

The reason I'm thinking about it today is that last night we talked to some friends, and the conversation revolved around parents with mental problems (it seems like in our friend's group, normal parents are the exception), and one friend said he has no contact with his mom. She apparently has a borderline personality disorder, and he cut all contact with her when he was young and refused any future attempts by her to reconnect. And I found myself thinking that it must be the dad's fault, that he didn't make any effort to help him with the connection (I don't know, maybe he was afraid of her, I'm not judging). I'm pretty sure that even if she was unfit as a mother and a wife, he still could have stayed in some kind of contact with her.

So, from myself and Dalia, and especially Dad, I would like to thank you for letting Dad be as much of a father to us as he was able to be.

You know it's not my usual habit to write heart-to-heart letters, so excuse me if it's not a great one. I would have attached a tissue pack, but mine is almost empty.

Happy Mother's Day,

Love Nitsan.

Of Cars and Dogs

August 2016

I turned into the small, tree lined street and examined the fenced mansions that loomed behind closed gates. Waiting in the air-conditioned car, I tried fishing in my jet-lagged foggy brain for the name and significance of the person whose house I was parked in front of, to no avail.

A dusty Renault pulled up behind me and to my relief, my sister stepped out.

"Hey, what's up?" We hugged briefly, "Impressive house, eh?" She tilted her head toward the property with mock admiration.

"Remind me who this guy is?" I asked apologetically.

"Yaakov? He was with dad in the kibbutz class, he's the one Yair said we should talk to, the guy who told a good story after the funeral?"

I was collecting my video recording equipment from the trunk when a husky man approached us from inside the gate. He was wearing a black T-shirt, his white hair pulled back in a ponytail, and with his white beard reminded me of Hemingway in his later years.

"You must be Saul's girls," he greeted us. "Can I help you carry anything?"

Once inside, he went to get us some cold water and I examined the yard for a shady spot to film the interview. While I set up my equipment, he asked us all the obligatory questions of where we lived and how many kids we had, then told us about himself, his high-ranking engineering job in the aviation industry and his successful children. b

When I was ready with the camera, he took his seat and began his monologue:

"I have two stories to tell you about Saul. The first happened..."

"Wait," I interrupted, "can you start with how you met?"

"Sure, sure," he said, and shifted a bit in his chair.

"I grew up in the city, in a fairly affluent family. When I was 16, I had a crush on my Youth Movement Leader who was from Ein Arava, and I convinced my parents to let me join the kibbutz. It wasn't an easy transition, and Saul, who was my classmate, volunteered to be my unofficial "liaison" and show me around.

We found each other by chance. I was a chess player from an early age, I took lessons, belonged to a club and competed in tournaments. One day, shortly after I arrived on the kibbutz, I saw Saul playing chess with Shlomo Kadosh, another classmate. I sat down to watch them. Their playing level was pretty basic and I asked to play against them. Obviously, I won. They were surprised. They were considered good players on the kibbutz, but I had thousands of hours of games in much larger settings.

Saul was an extraordinary kid. Exceptionally smart. But you probably know that. I met thousands of people in my life, and if I had to grade them according to their sharpness, he would always be at the top. First place."

Yaakov stopped for a moment to take a sip of water, and brush an invisible particle off his sleeve.

"And here is this new kid, beats him in chess easily, and he liked it." Yaakov continued. "You'd think he would be upset but not at all. On the contrary. Our class was, how to say it nicely... populated with not-too-smart kids. Smart people don't have much tolerance for the less intelligent, so Saul and Shlomo were happy to meet another kid on their level. That's how we became friends, Shlomo, Saul and I, connected by our intellect.

Saul, specifically, had zero tolerance for people who weren't smart. Many times, he replied to them impatiently. I remember how I would ask Saul about people in the kibbutz, and he would either say 'that's an interesting person' or 'don't bother with him' making a face. In general, he had a rough personality, he was big and tough in his behavior. He wasn't well liked by the rest of the class, but the three of us got on well together. After a few months they also began to win some chess games.

So that was how we became friends, but later, there were 2 specific events that solidified our friendship.

The first story happened towards the end of Junior year in high school. One evening, we came back with the rest of our class from watching a play at a neighboring kibbutz. The transport truck dropped us off at "The Circle," that was the nickname for the parking lot and drop-off point at the kibbutz entrance. We began walking toward our rooms, when Saul caught up with me, stopped me and said 'Listen, I saw the Command Car of the bee-keeping farm with the key in the switch. Let's take it for a ride."

"You know what a Command-Car is?" Yaakov paused from his story to ask us. "It's an army style, open-top all-terrain vehicle. They used them in the kibbutz for transportation to the fields and agricultural farms.

I told Saul he was out of his mind, but he persisted. He walked beside me and kept saying 'let's do it, come on' and finally he said: 'I'll let you drive too, I'll teach you to drive'. That's what convinced me. I admit, I was weak. kibbutz kids always had opportunities to drive, mostly agricultural equipment, but I grew up in the city and never did. We went back to the Circle, made sure no one was there, Saul sat at the wheel, started the vehicle and we drove out of the kibbutz and toward the fields.

Then he stopped the car and said 'Okay, your turn.' He showed me the gear stick and the clutch and explained how to use them. After a few failed tries I managed to get the car into gear and drive. I drove for a couple of miles and suddenly we saw a few people, 4 or 5, walking towards us, carrying stuff. I didn't know what to do, but Saul didn't hesitate. He said, 'Slow down and be ready to step on it' and I slowed down. They moved to the side, expecting us to stop for them, but instead, as soon as we passed them, I stepped on it, and we sped away. We heard the people yelling after us, but we kept going. Later we found out that it was the beehive farmers whose other vehicle got stuck in the mud a few miles away from the kibbutz and they had no choice but to walk back. They were so happy to see someone coming towards them, hoping for a ride, but we ran away.

We drove back to the kibbutz, and on the way, Saul told me that those were the beekeeping people, the ones who usually use that vehicle, and that we're in deep shit. At the entrance to the kibbutz, he stopped to let me get off, and I ran to my room to hide. The people we saw figured it must be teenagers who stole the car, and two of them ran through a short-cut directly to the teen dorms and began going from room to room to see who was missing. I hid under my blanket pretending to sleep and they didn't notice anything. The others went to the parking circle and caught Saul when he came back. They asked him who was with him but he didn't tell. He insisted it was just him.

They beat him up, hard. Physical violence wasn't a thing in the kibbutz, but this time they really hit him. He didn't talk. Didn't say a word. It was clear that if it came out that it was me, I'd be expelled from the kibbutz. The kibbutz members will think of me as the bad seed coming from the city to corrupt their good boys. Go tell them it was Saul who convinced me to join him.

They didn't let him go. They kept him all night, but he didn't tell them who was with him. The next day he was called to the school principal and was banned from going on the next overnight school trip as punishment, but he never told anybody I was with him. It remained our secret and solidified our friendship. I admired how he handled the beating; his loyalty. I doubt that if I was in his place, I would have kept quiet. A few months later, I had the opportunity to reciprocate, to be there for him when he needed help.

I think it was the beginning of our senior year when Saul adopted a puppy. A little thing, a Poodle, I believe. Very cute as puppies always are. They were inseparable. He carried her everywhere. I don't remember ever seeing her walking on her own. He hid her under his coat and took her with him to the Dining Room or to class, even though it was forbidden. He hand-fed her, let her sleep in his bed. It's hard to describe in words that kind of love and devotion, like a father to his firstborn. And, of course, she returned the love. Having that puppy also made him more popular in school; everybody wanted to pet her.

A few months later, the puppy developed some kind of skin rash. Her hair fell out, and she was covered in sores. Saul was really upset about it.

He went with her to a veterinarian who came to take care of the kibbutz's herd of cows to ask for his opinion. He gave him some powder to apply on her skin, but it only made it worse. A week later, I went with him to the vet again. He looked at her and said, "you need to kill her." I remember Saul shouting, 'No way!' But the veterinarian explained to him she's suffering, and if he loves her, he should take pity on her and end her pain. You could visibly see Saul's internal struggle, but he always listened to logic and understood what must be done. But he couldn't do it himself.

A couple of days later, I offered to do it for him. He said no. A day passed, then two, and eventually, he came to me and said, 'OK.'

I gave him three conditions. First, no one is to know about it. Second, he will not ask, and I will not tell him "how." Third, I will bury her and will not tell him where. My reasoning was I needed to help him get over that experience and not allow him to wallow in it. He agreed. That evening he brought her to me wrapped in a pillowcase. And he also gave me a shovel. I made him promise not to follow me, and I left. I came back after half an hour, and he waited for me. He didn't say anything, just looked at me with big question marks in his eyes, and I nodded. He came over and hugged me. I was a small kid at the time, he was much bigger, and he hugged me and didn't let go. I felt him trembling, and he began to cry. We stood like that for minutes, an hour, a day, an eternity... I don't know. He sobbed, and I held him." Yaakov stopped and swallowed hard. Reliving the memory, he had tears in his eyes.

"We never talked about it again." he continued. "I can only guess what he felt, how this experience affected him. As for me, it was like an initiation ritual, like the kids in Africa that need to go through a frightening experience to show courage. I came out of it a different person. We were about to join the army, and this experience of taking a life made me believe that I can face anything. As for our friendship, it became even stronger than before, and it remained that way."

"So, you kept in touch after the army?" Dalia asked, hopeful. "It's a period we don't have a lot of information about."

"Well...there was this time he got involved with some criminals; he left the kibbutz and was a currier for stolen goods. Do you know about that part?"

"No, not really," I said.

Although I wasn't familiar with this specific incident, I wasn't overly surprised. Dad often showed disregard for the written law. It usually involved the unauthorized use of motor vehicles, but there were other digressions over the years. From my experience, a person in a manic state is a bit like a teenager, unconcerned with rules, regulations, or consequences.

An article in Psychiatry Online about Bipolar Disorder and the Judiciary System adds that "the transgressions and criminal acts are typically associated with the manic phases of bipolar disorder, which are marked by irritability, exalted mood, and increased energy. These phases are often associated with megalomaniac ideas and feelings of omnipotence that could lead to public order offenses or confrontations with the police."

The afternoon sun had moved, and a patch of light was now bleaching out the edge of Yaakov's green chair, creeping close to his face. I used the break between the stories to readjust the camera frame, directing Yaakov to shift his chair a few inches left.

"Can you tell this story from the beginning? About his involvement with the criminals?"

I asked when I had him in focus again.

"I was already married. We lived on the Hatzor army base, in the family housing unit. He called me from Bilu and said that the police are looking for him. I drove there, picked him up, and brought him to the base with me. I figured the police were not going to look for him in an army base. He stayed with us for a few days. I called Shlomo Kadosh. People from the kibbutz were looking for him. We convinced him to go back, I think. I'm not sure exactly what happened after."

"Can you estimate approximately when it was? What year?" I asked, trying to fit this new piece of information into our patchwork puzzle.

"Let me think...." Yaakov said, "I got married in 68, so it was probably 69 or 1970."

"Do you think he was manic then?" Dalia asked

Yaakov hesitated, "No...I don't think so. I think he left the kibbutz and needed a way to make money and somehow got involved with some people who took advantage of his abilities."

Yaakov paused, his gaze fixed on the empty space between us, but his mind was focused forty five years in the past. We waited.

"I was in the army those years, but Shlomo told me about what happened in Karameh. He was one of the first people to recognize that something was wrong. He took care of him, got him hospitalized. Later, maybe it was 1970, I visited him once in the Talbiya hospital, but other than that we didn't keep in touch."

Driving away, the mansions of Caesarea getting smaller in my rear-view mirror, I couldn't help but compare Yaakov's home to my dad's meager apartment and wonder whether in a parallel universe in which Karameh never happened, my dad is also living the life of a successful professional, fitting for the most brilliant guy Yaakov ever met.

Accident

1970

"**I** need to check something under the truck, don't touch anything, Okay, Tsani?" Dad says and climbs down from the cabin.

We are at the parking lot of some kibbutz in the south, where Dad needs to load apples from the orchard and bring them to a central packing facility.

I slouch on the large seat, it's warm, and the back of my legs in my shorts are getting sweaty against the black vinyl. I look out the window, a stray tabby jumps out of a trash bin and disappears behind the bushes. I'm bored. I have nothing to play with. Maybe I can pretend to be a truck driver, like Dad?

I grab the round plastic ball at the top of the long stick shift, the way I've seen Dad do when he's driving; I make truck sounds, "vroom, vroom," and move the pole around.

Suddenly, the engine roars to life, and the truck lurches forward, then stops. Did I hear a scream? I'm not sure.

I huddle in the seat, hugging my legs to my chest and burying my face in my knees. Tears run down my leg mixing with the sweat.

A few minutes pass, but I don't dare to move. Finally, Dad pulls open the truck's cabin door. His pants are ripped and smeared with dirt and blood.

I whimper, "I didn't do anything!"

He is quiet. I can see he's upset. When he notices my wet face, he says, "It's okay, nothing happened, I'm fine, but let's go to the clinic to get it checked."

Every kibbutz has a medical clinic that serves the members, staffed by nurses experienced in treating minor injuries and common afflictions. Luckily, it's not far.

We enter the clinic and find a nurse. It's someone Dad knows, and she is surprised to see him. She instructs me to sit in the waiting area, and Dad follows her into the treatment room.

When they emerge, Dad's leg bulges under the jeans, and the rip in the pants is held together with medical tape.

"Do you like my new style?" He jokes. "I'm okay. The nurse bandaged my leg. It's just a big bruise."

The nurse follows him into the waiting room.

She is a large person; she hovers over me (or at least that's how I remember it), her face stern, and says, "You know you could have killed your dad there? Don't ever do something like that again. You're very lucky it ended up this way."

When we're out of the building and far enough from the scary nurse, I stop and ask, "Is it true what she said? That I almost killed you?"

"Nah," Dad laughs, "if you really wanted to run me over, you would have pressed on the gas pedal."

Mirror

1972-3

After my parents' divorce, we stayed at Ein Arava, my dad's kibbutz. My mom worked as an elementary school teacher, my sister and I lived in the Children's House, and my father, between hospitalizations, was mostly working as a truck driver in Jerusalem or Tel-Aviv.

When I was 6, my mom met Dubi, a tall, handsome medical student from another kibbutz, and they fell in love right away. They began dating, and when my mom got pregnant, they decided to marry.

One February morning, I woke up early and noticed that Aviv, one of my 3 roommates, was tossing and turning in his bed.

"Aviv," I whispered, "Are you awake?"

The sleeping schedule at the children's house was very strict. Lights-off time was never changed and closely observed. Once the lights were off, we were expected to stay quietly in bed until we fell asleep. Talking or moving around earned us a stern reproach. The same was true for the morning wake-up. If a child woke up before the official wake-up time, they were expected to stay quietly in bed until the caretaker announced it was time to get up.

Aviv turned toward me and whispered something back. "What?" I asked and mustered the courage to sit up. We chatted in hushed voices for a few minutes when we heard footsteps approaching our room. We ducked back under the covers to pretend we were sleeping as the caretaker opened the door.

"Nitsan," she said, and I realized I was caught. Maybe if I stayed quietly under the covers, I could still fool her?

"Nitsan, congratulations, you have a baby sister!" She said and went to open the shades, signaling to the rest of the children that it was time to wake up.

I sat up in bed, confused. Mom wasn't due for another month. She and Dubi went for an unexpected medical test yesterday afternoon, or so we were told, and Dalia and I spent the afternoon hours at our grandparents' place.

"Really?" I jumped out of bed and twirled a little happy dance, then skipped to the communal bathroom for teeth brushing while announcing to the children I passed on the way the great news.

* * *

Several months after Efrat was born, our newly formed family left my dad's kibbutz and temporarily relocated to kibbutz Assif in the Judaean Mountains. My stepfather Dubi was studying medicine in Jerusalem, a three-hour bus ride from Ein Arava, and the move would allow him to come home every day. Years later, when I interviewed my uncle Yair, he told me that there was another reason. My father's family had a hard time seeing my mom move on and requested that she leave. Whatever the reason was, we moved to the new kibbutz four days before the beginning of second grade.

On the day we arrived, my mom took me to meet my new caretaker and classmates and see the Children's House.

The new kibbutz was much smaller than the kibbutz I grew up in. There were only 11 kids in my class, about half of my previous group. We shared the Children's House with the first graders. In the mundane routine of kibbutz life, the arrival of a new kid was a novelty. Excited, the group gathered around me, some checking me out quietly, a few venturing to say hi.

"Liat," said Stella, the caretaker, a large woman with short curly hair and an American accent, "Show Nitsan the Children's House, her bed and cubby."

A pretty girl with long black hair stepped up and took me by the hand, "Come."

My mom lingered for a few minutes, talking to the caretaker, then came after me to see my bed, gave me a quick hug, and said she'll be back in the afternoon to take me to our new "room" and left.

During summer vacation, kibbutz children still lived in the Children's House. Our schedule wasn't that different than during school time, other than the fact that there were no classes. On some days, we had organized activities like The Olympics when we competed against other grades in Field Day games or Indian Day in which we all dressed up like storybook Native Americans and participated in what our camp counselors considered typical activities. But most of the days were spent at the swimming pool, where I found myself the following day.

I was sitting with two of my new classmates on what was supposed to be a lawn but was now a patchy, mostly dry sprawl of grass, with occasional grass burrs, eating sweet grapes out of an orange plastic bowl, trying not to bite down on the bitter seeds.

"Hey, you're the new girl, aren't you?" Three older boys were standing behind us. I was startled, realizing they were talking to me.

"What's your name?"

"Nitsan," I mumbled.

"Nitsan? That's a boy's name, are you a boy?" said the tall one with a smirk on his face. I was pretty sure that with my long hair and full bathing suit, I looked nothing like a boy.

"It's also a girl's name! Stupid" Liat, next to me, came to my rescue.

"You're stupid, hanging out with the new boy," his friend, short and sunburned, yelled as they ran away, laughing.

"Don't mind them; you have a beautiful name," said Liat. She was one of those girls who acted mature from an early age, which is also probably, why she had taken it upon herself to hang out with the "new girl."

The boys were right, though. At the time, Nitsan, meaning "flower bud," was primarily known in Israel as a boy's name. In the kibbutz where I grew up, everybody knew me from an early age, so my name was never a subject of surprise or mocking. Here I was in a new territory and an easy target for missiles of children's cruelty.

That night, lying in bed, I decided to change my name to Rose. It was such a nice, ordinary name, unquestionably girly. On the first day of school, I wrote Rose on all my notebooks.

There's a life-changing quality in moving to a new place as a child, especially if you grew up in a small community where everybody knew you. I'm not talking about leaving behind your friends or learning the geography of a new neighborhood. I'm talking about the feeling of self. For me, the move felt like I was seeing myself in the mirror for the first time. Because of my young age, the things I saw were primarily superficial, like my unusual name or the large scar I had in my abdomen from surgery. Things my previous classmates were used to and allowed me to forget, and here brought on curiosity and frequent comments.

Also, here, no one knew about my family's situation. On my dad's kibbutz, everybody knew my family and our history better than I did. The adults knew my dad as a young, healthy man and later, heard of, or saw him in a manic episode, or maybe even actively participated in restraining him or searching for me when he took me without permission. Most of them probably had an opinion too:

"The poor guy, he showed such promise." "Tragic Deborah

and Ezra, they already have one disabled son, and now this." "Pity for Alona, such a nice young couple, she doesn't deserve it." "What a bitch, a few problems and she abandons him for some good- looking medical student."

Whatever their viewpoint was, kind or judging, they had one. It's embedded in the matrix of any kibbutz.

Here, on the new kibbutz, I had an opportunity, a decision to make. Do I tell anybody about my father? And if I do, how much? So, in theory, no one had to know, as long as my dad didn't visit. And even if they knew that Dubi wasn't my real father, they didn't have to know about my dad's illness. And yet, as a child, I don't think the idea of lying, hiding, omitting the truth even crossed my mind.

From the time I could understand, or even before that, both my parents were very open about the disease and the divorce. They told me Dad had a traumatic experience during an army operation, and because of that, he became mentally ill with something called Manic Depressive Disorder. They also said that mental illness, like any other illness, is nothing to be ashamed of or hide. Liat, who became my best friend in my new class, was the first one I told.

War

October 6, 1973

I woke up from a deep sleep with a startle and forced my eyes open, unsure what time or day it was. The direct sunlight filtering through the shades clued me in. It was afternoon. Then I became aware of the noise. Was it a siren? Why? And how come the other kids didn't wake up from it?I slithered over to Sigal's bed and grabbed her shoulder through the thin blanket.

"Sigal, wake up, Sigal!"

She opened her eyes. "There's a siren. What's happening?"

Gal and Eli, our roommates, also woke up and joined us on my bed - huddled over.

It was Saturday afternoon in the kibbutz's Children's House. Naptime. We were expected to sleep or at least stay quiet in our beds until we were told it's time to get up. Despite the siren, we tried to be as noiseless as we could. The Saturday caretaker was a young woman we didn't know very well, and we were afraid she might be the angry-yelling type.

There she was at the door. We all crept back to our beds, but she didn't seem piqued, just sad. She sat on the corner of my bed and said, "Did you hear the sirens?" We all nodded silently. "There's a war. A war has started. They said on the radio that Egypt and Syria both attacked us this morning...»

"But there's no radio today; it's Yom Kippur," Eli, the know-it-all interrupted. Yom Kippur is the Jewish day of atonement. It's the holiest day in the Jewish tradition. We all knew that since Israel defines itself as a Jewish State, all businesses are closed on that day, and there are no radio or television broadcasts.

By now, children that were sleeping in the other rooms joined us.

"You're right," said the caretaker, "usually there isn't any news. That's what the sirens are for, to let us know. The radio is broadcasting – they have to give updates on the fighting and information for soldiers so they know where to join their units. All the soldiers, including those on reserve duty, must leave as soon as possible."

We sat there, listening to the siren that kept blaring outside, rolling the word "war" on our tongues, examining it, tasting it. What does it mean to us? How will it affect our lives? The predominant flavor was dread. We never experienced war ourselves, but we'd heard about them and we knew that war was bad. But there was something else, another flavor mixed in with it, a sweetness, a hidden hint of excitement, adventure.

Heavy footsteps could be heard in the hallway, and Eli's dad walked in, dressed in an olive army uniform and carrying a heavy-looking khaki duffle bag. He was soon followed by a procession of fathers who stopped by the Children's House to kiss their kids goodbye before catching transportation to their army reserve units. When the last of the men left, we children remained to contemplate the situation.

We gathered in one of the bedrooms and sat on the beds.

"I'm afraid," someone said. "What if the Egyptians come here and capture us?"

"There's no way. Our army is the best, the strongest; we will crush them," a boy said with typical Israeli bravado.

"But they can bomb us from airplanes."

"Nah, our tanks will shoot them down!"

"I'm scared my dad will get killed," someone said, which initiated a cascade of murmurs full of "what ifs."

As second graders, we were probably way too young to comprehend the death of a parent and too embarrassed to cry, so we kept the conversation going, somber and composed.

Since my father was no longer part of the army reserve due to his mental illness, I knew that he was out of harm's way.

So, instead, I added my favorite uncle to the conversation.

War II

October 6, 1973

Saul stood at the window of his Tel-Aviv Apartment and watched the roads that two hours earlier were utterly empty fill up with droves of Uzi-carrying soldiers dashing down the streets leading to the Central Bus Station. A beat-up Susita station wagon double-parked right under his window. A young woman, ignoring the cars honking behind her, got out of the driver's seat and walked over to hug the soldier who was extracting a heavy bag from the trunk. She seemed reluctant to let him go as he returned a brief hug, then hurried away, and she finally noticed she was blocking the lane and drove on.

In Saul's room, the radio announcer repeated the report: "Since two o'clock this afternoon the Egyptian and Syrian armies have been attacking our army bases in the Sinai Desert and the Golan Heights, on the ground and from the air. Our forces are returning fire." This message was followed by a stream of unit codes and meeting places, then instructions on darkening all residential windows to make it harder for enemy bombers to aim at densely populated centers. The name of his unit was called, grabbing his attention, but he had nowhere to go. He was no longer a soldier; he didn't even have a uniform.

At 6 pm, the stream of public announcements was halted for Prime Minister Golda Meir's address to the nation, and Saul realized that he's out of cigarettes. He went downstairs to the neighborhood kiosk, and when he got there, discovered with annoyance that his roommate had stolen his last 100 Liras before he left for the war.

The following days went by quickly. He worked long hours, covering for the drafted drivers, taking on as many deliveries as he could, and sleeping very little. At night he roamed the darkened, deserted city streets. At least then, there was no one to look at him with accusation, wondering why an able-bodied young man is working in Tel-Aviv while their son or husband is somewhere fighting or worse.

On October 14th, the army began to notify the families of the dead. Printed black frames broke out on city surfaces. His dad called and told him of the soldiers from the kibbutz who were killed in the fighting so far, and he felt a deep shame. Shame that he was at home while they were dying out there.

When he opened his apartment door on the evening of October 15th, he saw army boots on the floor and uniforms draped on a chair. The thieving bastard roommate came for vacation and was sleeping, probably exhausted, in his bed. Without thinking about it too much, Saul emptied the army bag and packed it with his own stuff. Years of army service coming back like muscle memory. He undressed, put on the mate's uniform and boots, shouldered his Uzi, and quietly closed the door behind him.

He rode his Vespa south all night. At dawn, he stopped at a gas station for coffee and cigarettes. The man at the counter pushed back his money and a whole carton of cigarettes and said, "Here, bring some cigarettes to your friends; it's on us; we are honored to serve our brave soldiers." Saul thanked him and drove on.

A Box of Oranges

2016

Both Professor Ginath and My uncle Yair suggested that we talk to Avi Rimon, an army major who fought in Karameh and a member of "Ein Arava," my dad's kibbutz. Dalia contacted Avi, and he agreed to speak with us.

Since Avi knew Dad from the kibbutz, and was in the same army unit, we hoped he could tell us more about what happened during the Karameh battle.

We made a quick stop at our grandmother's house to say hi, then drove to the other side of the kibbutz to Avi's place.

He waited for us outside, a man of average height, with a slight bulging in his midriff, his skin a light grayish brown, speckled with age spots, the type of tan a light-skinned person gets from years of working in the fields. He was dressed in a khaki button-down shirt open halfway and shorts, a large mustache balancing out his receding hairline. He invited us to sit outside on the patio, explaining that his wife is cooking the Friday night family dinner inside. A whiff of fried chicken cutlets that escaped through the window confirmed.

We arranged chairs and the camera, Avi buttoned up his shirt, and I began by asking him where and when he first remembers Dad.

"Let me start by saying that it's been 50 years, 50 years is a long time, although look, even the Germans are only now starting to write about World War II, the serious literature is only now being published, or here, now everybody writes about the

Yom Kippur war, things that we, the upper command, knew back then but nobody talked about." He pauses for a second, then continues, his tone dark, heavy. "Yom Kippur angers me so much," he looks down and shakes his head like he's trying to loosen up a thought that got snagged on a rusting memory. "So much...it was such a fiasco, we lost so many soldiers...my brother... and I keep thinking...."

The door to the house opens behind him; his wife, thin, in a floral housedress, steps out, but when she sees that we are already recording, she glides back in. The distraction interrupts Avi's digression, and when we start again, he returns to my question.

"You asked how I knew Saul. I knew him first from the kibbutz, from the school. I was a few years older than him. In the kibbutz's school, the kids of the upper classes acted as Youth Leaders for the lower classes, and I was assigned to his class. Twice a week, in the evenings, I took them out for activities...." Here he deviates again, describing some of the typical activities of those evenings, his difficulties with the task of being a youth leader, but eventually comes back to the topic.

"Saul was a brilliant guy; it was obvious that he knew things. From reading... I don't know, from his father? Ezra was something else; you remember him? Used to work in the vegetable fields, he had that slow, wobbly gait, always talking to himself with those hand motions, very smart, very well-read...."

Avi stops for a sip of water, and I ask, "You were together in the army, right?"

"Yes, yes, not together; he was my soldier. I was a company commander in the paratroopers brigade, and Saul, after his discharge from regular service in the Shaked unit, was assigned to my company for reserve duty. Not just him, but a large group of soldiers from elite units. On his first day, I called him aside and said, "I remember you, you're a wise guy, are you going to give me trouble?" And he said, "No, no, no, I promise," and here Avi raises his hand, demonstrating an 'I swear' motion, and I notice that he is missing the tip of his left ring finger.

"Now Saul, in the army, like in high school, was obviously brilliant and knowledgeable but also had a big mouth. He was in excellent physical shape, strong. He knew the names of all the birds and the flowers. Like my wife... anywhere in the world that we go, she points out the names of the birds; who cares? I tried to argue with him sometimes, but he was always right. He was a good soldier. Many years later, when I began to read about IDF (Israeli Defense Force) history, I understood the level of training he got there in Shaked.

"It's hard to be a commander, especially a company commander of soldiers from your own kibbutz, and more so if you are close in age. As long as it's just training and running on the dunes, it's fun; let's see who's faster. But when you go into battle, and someone might get hurt, I, as a commander, and I don't know about others because we never talked about it, but if it was someone from Ein Arava, I tried to keep them away from me. From danger. You know, only in the IDF you hear about so many causalities among higher-ranking soldiers. You know why? Because the IDF is embedded with the 'after me' culture, the officers charge ahead. And when you're first, you're more likely to get hurt."

"Was Dad in your platoon in The Six Day War?" Dalia asks.

"Yes. He was," Avi thinks for a second, "He was, but I don't remember anything specific. In March of '68, we went to Karameh. We were initially by the Allenby Bridge, and then my platoon was told to go to the Damia Bridge in preparation to enter Jordan. I remember the feeling, a chill down my spine, cold sweat on my back, I knew it was going to be very dangerous, and I made the decision, I instructed the two guys I knew from Ein Arava, Saul, and Amir, who became my brother-in-law," Avi makes a hand motion in the direction of Amir's house, just beyond the hedge, "to stay behind with the other platoon."

"At the end, we didn't enter Jordan, and when we came back, I heard about Saul's collapse. You see someone who is physically strong and confident, and you expect them to also be mentally resilient. But Saul, when he was sent to collect the body of a soldier into a sleeping bag, a grain of the disease that was in him flared up. It broke him. He never talked to me about it; that's what Ginath later explained to me. After that, he didn't go to reserve duty anymore."

It seems like this is all Avi knows about Karameh, and I'm disappointed. Coming here, we thought Avi might know more details about what happened to Dad, not just what Ginath told him. Still, maybe he could direct us to who might know more. But before I can ask, he continues.

"Do you know the story about him on Yom Kippur?" I shake my head and tilt it in a 'please go on' gesture.

"It was what? 5 years later? During the Yom Kippur war, I was already deputy battalion commander. My battalion was on the front lines, the first to cross the Suez Canal, on October 15 or 16. It was after 10 days of fighting and many casualties, and we were there for over 30 hours by ourselves, a couple of hundred soldiers, with only seven tanks. The history books talk about 21 tanks, but they are wrong. Fourteen were still on the other side and only seven had crossed. Suddenly, we see a tank transporter drive up, crossing the bridge over the canal, the bed empty with no tanks, just something covered with a tarp in the back, and Saul waves at us from the cabin." Avi raises both hands and mimics a wide, enthusiastic hand gesture. "He was across the canal already. He got down from the cabin, took down his Vespa, took down a box of oranges, and said, "I am here to join you!"

"Of course, we sent him back. We couldn't... Today, looking back, maybe if there was someone there who better understood the human mind, perhaps we would have acted differently, but when you're under fire, in the middle of a war, and it's someone you know, especially someone you know... it gets complicated. I couldn't have him there, so we sent him back. Next time I saw him was here, on the kibbutz."

A car drives on the road behind us, and I use the momentary break to digest what he just told us. Dad crossed the Suez Canal. On a tank transporter? 'The Crossing of the Canal,' as it's referred to, a legendary event in Israeli military history, the turning point of the Yom Kippur war, the subject of numerous books, and we had no idea? I'm tempted to ask him if he is sure, if there is anybody else who can corroborate this story, but I don't. He seems convinced enough, and I like the story too much to risk losing it to doubt.

When the car passed by and we resume, Dalia asks him again if he remembers any other details about Karameh, but he doesn't. He tries to remember who the other platoon commander was but he's not sure. He mentions a couple of possible names, and Dalia writes them down.

"Do you think there were any signs of his illness before Karameh?" I ask.

"As far as I could see, no. He worked hard at the vegetable farm; I would have known if there were any issues; he was as dedicated as a dog. He did some stupid things, stole vehicles and stuff, but it's something that kibbutz teens do. During the service before Karameh, he was a trustworthy soldier, the guy I knew was always properly prepared, always at the front, a strong guy who could carry an extra load. Only after that incident, can you imagine what a 30 tons tank does to a human body? It flattens it completely. And even though I wasn't there, these were my soldiers; I was responsible for them."

"Did anybody talk about PTSD then?" I asked.

"No, we didn't know it existed. We had the overconfidence of young men, paratroopers; we saw ourselves as invincible."

He looks around and suddenly seems restless, "Are we done?

Do you have any more questions? I really don't remember anything else."

I say no, I think this is it, but before I turn off the camera, he says, "You know, in the last few years, I sometimes saw Deborah or Yair going to see him, bringing him food. I never talked to Deborah about it, I imagined it would be too hard for her, but I asked Yair. I also went to visit Saul a couple of times. I know that he usually didn't welcome visitors, but with me, I guess he felt some connection because he let me in.

Of course, I was at the funeral, and after that, I said to some friends that I think it was very respectable. There were a lot of people, and the things that were read were to the point. Especially you. One would have thought that you would abandon him, but you didn't."

In the following days, we tracked down the guy that Avi thought may have been the other platoon commander. Dalia spoke to him, but he said it wasn't him. As far as he remembered, it was another guy, who died several years ago when he hit a wild boar on the road late at night.

A Trip to the Movies

October 1973

On October 25th, a cease-fire was agreed upon and the Yom Kippur War came to an end. A few days later, my dad showed up one afternoon at the kibbutz and offered to take my sister and me to see a film in Jerusalem.

My mom hesitated, but Dad seemed to be stable and promised to bring us back before dinner. We, of course, were ecstatic. It was a rare treat for girls from the kibbutz to go to the movies in the city, and there was also a mention of ice cream.

My dad parked the truck in a parking lot near the center of Jerusalem, and we stepped into the cool fall afternoon, the Jerusalem stone buildings looming majestically above us. The air was filled with foreign scents of car exhaust, cat urine and the sweet smell of roasting coffee from the nearby coffee shop. Close by were four movie theaters, and we walked towards them to see what was showing.

We stopped at the first ice cream stand we passed and bought two cones of chocolate-vanilla soft serve.

Dad handed us the cones and said, "Wait, I need to taste it first to make sure it's not poison."

We each let him have a spoonful, smiling with anticipation. He took a moment then said, "Hmm... I'm not sure... I need another bite." Again, we each gave him a spoonful, and he made a show of serious consideration then said with a straight face, "I'm still not hundred percent convinced it's safe; I think I might require another bite." We giggled at the familiar tease, then dug into the ice cream ourselves while he lit a cigarette.

We continued down the street, checking the movie posters in the theater windows, looking for the colorful telltale of children's features. A drawing of a smiling pig, surrounded by other animals and humans, caught my eye. The heading read "The Magic Farm" (the Hebrew name given to *Charlotte's Web*). We all agreed to see it.

When the movie ended, we left the theater singing the theme song, or something close to it, as we skipped back to the parking lot.

We got to the truck, and my dad took out the keys. Come, I tugged at my sister's arm and began to walk around to the passenger door when a voice behind us said, "Excuse me, sir, is that your truck?"

Two uniformed soldiers approached us.

I held my sister's hand and signaled her to stay quiet. One of the soldiers took out a badge and said, "Military police. Is that your truck?"

"Yes, I'm driving it," my father feigned nonchalance. "Is there a problem?"

"Are you a soldier?" Asked the female MP.

"Yes, of course. I'm home for vacation, just took my little girls to the movies." He said while gesturing in our general direction.

My sister sniffled, and I shot her a warning stare. This was no time to act like a baby.

The MPs asked to see his soldier's I.D.

Dad took his time, taking a long drag on his cigarette, then crushing it under the sole of his shoe while flicking away some ash that fell into his beard. He casually took his wallet out from his back pocket and pretended to check for the document.

For a moment even I fell for his show of casual confidence, expecting him to produce the required proof somehow.

"I'm sorry, I must have left it at home," he mumbled, still leafing through the meager contents.

It was early evening, the sun stooped behind the tall buildings, leaving the street drained of color. A woman passing by slowed to look at our unusual party.

I stared down, examining the cracks and cavities in the asphalt beneath my feet.

"Sir, we will have to ask you to come with us," said the soldier.

"Why? What did I do? What about my girls?"

Dalia pulled her hand out of mine and ran over to Dad, hugging his leg. He lifted her up, and she hid her face in his shoulder.

"Sir, this is a seized Egyptian army truck. It belongs in a confiscated equipment lot; it doesn't belong on the road. We don't know how you got hold of it, but we can't let you drive it any further, and you will need to come with us. Is there someone who can pick up your daughters?"

Dad signaled to me to come closer, crouched to my height, and explained that everything was okay, but he did something stupid, and he needs to go with the soldiers to sort it out. I hugged him and inhaled his familiar smokey scent. Then, like the big girl I was, I let him go.

He waved over a taxi and paid him to take us back to the kibbutz.

From the back seat, Dalia and I watched as our dad sheepishly followed the MPs to the police car. Despite his attempts to reassure us, it was clear to me that he was being handled like a criminal just because he wanted to treat us to some fun. How I wished I had the power to protect him.

Blue Bear

1974

Iskipped barefoot down the narrow path, made a shortcut through the lawn, narrowly avoiding a small ant hill, and came to a halt a few feet from my parent's door. The large Khaki military bag on the front porch signaled that Dubi, my stepfather, was home from his army service.

My little sister saw me through the window and rushed out.

"Dubi is back; look what he got us; which one do you want?" She held two stuffed bears in both hands: a light blue one and a smaller brown one.

"Can I have the blue one?" she chirped, not waiting for an answer. Of course, she'd want the same one I did, but I was the older sister and was expected to let her choose. She thrust the scrawny brown bear in my direction. I ignored it, and as we walked into the house, I said "You know, Dubi is not our father. I don't want any gifts from him, and you shouldn't take them either!"

She dropped the brown bear on the floor and hugged the blue bear with both arms, as if protecting it from a vicious kidnapper. I attempted to pull it out of her grasp, but my mom intercepted us.

"Nits, what's going on? Why is she crying?" Statistically, she made the correct assumption. If my sister was crying, it was likely my doing.

"I told her Dubi isn't our father, and she shouldn't take gifts from him." I spat out.

My mom's face recoiled in pain for a split second, but she quickly recovered and gently ushered me to their bedroom, closed the door, and sat on the edge of the bed.

"Nitsani, what happened?" She intoned with her eternally patient voice.

"I hate Dubi; he's not my father; Dad is my father!" I yelled. She attempted to hug me, but I wiggled out.

"You know that Dad and I divorced a long time ago."

"You left him! He is sick, and you abandoned him! You shouldn't do that; you can't leave a sick person like that. You should divorce Dubi and marry Dad again." At 7, I was mature for my age and well-versed in relevant literature like Erich Kastner's "Lottie and Lisa," where the little girls convince their divorced parents to reconcile and remarry. The only obstacle, as I saw it, was Dubi.

"But Nits," she reached for me again, and noticing the wetness pooling in her eyes, I allowed her to hug me this time, "You know that Dad and I decided together to separate. When he got sick, he changed. The disease changed him. He was no longer the same person I married. We both talked about it and agreed that we no longer belong together," she recited the official version I grew up with. Did I already sense the deceit?

Not knowing how to answer that, I conceded defeat and allowed the bell to ring on round one in a match that would last well into my teens.

Cracks

1974

Who are you when you are seven or eight? Which hero or heroine do you identify with? Are you a Disney princess, pretty and delicate? And if you are, which princess are you? Sleeping Beauty? A victim of circumstances beyond her control, or are you Cinderella or Snow White, still pretty but not completely helpless, active participants in their rescue?

Or maybe you're a Tomboy, like Pippi Longstocking, climbing trees and riding horses, or a bespectacled nerd banished from ball games to protect your eyeglasses, the darling of the school librarian who lets you borrow books from the "older kids" section?

I fancied myself a warrior; out to defend my sick father against the evil stepfather who took his princess, his family. Not a sword-yielding fighter, but a strong, resilient promoter of justice. My role models were brave girls like Tamar, the deputy commander in the book series "The Absolutely Absolute Secret Group," "Anne Frank" and of course the twins Lottie and Lisa from Erich Kastner's book by that name (Better known to the American audience as the movie The Parent Trap).

My mission wasn't easy. The characters in my life story did not easily fit into the classic templates. Dad refused to be a victim. Together with my mom, he stuck with the explanation that their divorce was a mutual decision. He also was on friendly terms with Dubi and never had a bad word to say about him. Dubi didn't fit well into the evil stepdad mold either. He was a kind and gentle guy, always patient with us, a loving husband to my mom. And mom? How should I cast her? If she was bad, then I had nobody to rely on, no ally in the world. But can I let her off the hook?

When things at home were not great, the kibbutz offered an alternative in the form of the Children's House class. After all, we spent 21 hours of each day there, eating, sleeping, showering, studying, and playing. I assimilated well into "Yaara", which means honeysuckle (all kibbutz classes had names, usually of plants or trees), made good friends with the other children, especially the girls, and overall, was relatively popular. But even on the kibbutz, certain weaknesses would not be forgiven.

I woke up one night with a lukewarm wetness that was spreading under me. I lay quietly, threads of a dream still clinging to my mind, mixing in with an equally confusing reality. I slowly lifted my blanket and sniffed. The warm odor of fresh urine left no room for mistake; I'd peed myself. As a third grader in the Children's House, the stakes were clear. If any of my classmates were to find out about it, I'd be the target of their mockery and most likely the laughingstock of the entire elementary school for all eternity.

What should I do? Summoning the night-watcher was out of the question. There was no way I could call her from under the intercom box that was hanging up on the wall without waking up any of the other kids, and even if I managed to do that, she would probably make too much noise when she came into the room. Staying in a wet bed only meant delaying my eventual discovery until the morning. Not an option either.

I got up soundlessly and tiptoed to the Caretakers Room, where clean laundry for the entire class was arranged in white wooden cubicles. I chose a pajama set identical to the one I was wearing. That wasn't hard, all the children's pajamas were made 'at home,' meaning sewn on the kibbutz from wholesale bought patterned fabric, so there were always many similar sets. I picked a pair of underwear from the next cubby and went to the bathroom to change. Rinsing myself off was out of the question. The sound of running water in the shower will surely summon someone. An oversized laundry bag was hanging on a metal frame in the shower room, and I had to stand on my tippy toes to push my wet pajamas all the way to the bottom.

I went back to my room and examined my sheet by the faint glow of the nightlight. There was an obvious circle of wetness. I had to change it. I peeled it off the mattress and buried it next to the incriminating pajamas. At eight years old, I was rather adept at changing sheets. All kibbutz children changed their own beds once a week on a pre-determined day.

I slept little that night, waking up every so often to check that I hadn't peed myself again. By morning, the little moisture that remained in the mattress had evaporated almost entirely and the smell was undetectable amidst the aroma of four sweaty children in a small room.

I wet myself again that year. I'm not sure how many times or what caused it, but each time I handled it the same way, changing my pajamas and sheets by myself, burying the evidence deep in the laundry bag. No one ever found out. Not even the care-taker or my mom.

Later, as an adult, I learned that bed wetting in older children could be a sign of psychological distress. Was it a result of my family situation? Concern for my dad? Ambivalent emotions regarding Dubi and my mom? Was that a sign that under the strong facade, something was cracking?

Vespa

1974 or 1975

I was sitting at the breakfast table, examining with disgust the film floating on my cooling cup of hot chocolate and contemplating my options. Drinking it was out of the question, but I was afraid leaving the unfinished drink on the table would get me in trouble again. Our regular caretaker was away for the entire week, and we had a substitute, an older woman who believed children needed to "clean up" their plates and cups. On her first day, she made me stay at the table for a full hour after everyone went back to class, insisting I drink the milk despite the film on top, eventually releasing me with a 'last time' warning.

The front door of the Children's House opened with a screech, and an unfamiliar man entered. He stood in the hallway, scanning the little faces, and then, looking straight at me, a smile lit his eyes, and he began walking in my direction.

I stared, as he approached, convinced he had me confused with someone else when he stopped and said, "Hi Tsani!"

"Dad?" I said, struggling to reconcile the familiar voice with the clean-shaven face.

I pushed back my chair and jumped up to hug him.

"Are you done eating? I'll tell your teacher I'm taking you with me for a few hours," he said, and I took my cup and plate to the sink, emptying the leftovers into the trash, confident the caretaker would not say anything while my father was there.

We picked up my sister from her classroom and went to sit

on a bench swing nearby. Dad handed us chocolate bars, and I found it hard not to stare at his naked cheeks. For as long as I could remember, Dad had a full reddish beard.

"Look what I got printed yesterday," he said and handed us each a business card from a stack in his wallet. The cards were white and printed with blue letters:

Samuel P. Road Service
Fast and affordable service for cars, trucks, and motorcycles.

"Who's Samuel P.?" I asked?

"Me," Dad said. "It's just a name I use sometimes. I'm going to start a road service business. I'll drive around on my Vespa, and if I see a car stuck on the road, I'll stop and offer to help them for a fee. I can fix almost anything in a car, you know."

I was certainly impressed by the pile of identical mini cards, crisp and neatly printed. I didn't know anybody in the kibbutz who had business cards.

"Keep it," he said when I tried to hand it back. "Do you want to go on a ride? I can teach you how to drive."

We walked to the parking lot at the entrance to the kibbutz, and Dad showed us the wooden toolbox he fixed on the back of the Vespa.

"Who wants to drive? Tsani, do you mind if I take Dalia first?"

He sat on the Vespa and showed Dalia how to stand in front of him and hold the handlebar. He explained that on one side was the gas, and you turned it to drive faster, and the other side was the brake. He showed her how to put her little hands just next to his, and they slowly rolled away. I sat on a rock and waited. Time passed. A black dung beetle wobbled by, almost flipping over when attempting to scale a large clump of dry dirt. With the sole of my sandal, I smashed down the lumpy earth, flattening the ground and clearing a flat path in front of her, but the stupid creature ignored my benevolent offering and turned another way.

I walked around, trying to find a vantage point that would allow me to survey the main road, but they were nowhere in sight. I picked up a large stone and watched a hotchpotch of critters scamper away from the sudden sunlight when I finally heard the roar of the Vespa approaching.

I ran towards them. Dad stopped the Vespa next to me and, with a big smile, announced, "Dalia is a natural-born driver. Now your turn." He lifted her from her waist with both hands and placed her on the ground, then motioned for me to climb up. He repeated the explanation about the gas and the brake and told me to turn the handle gently.

I yelled to Dalia, "Just wait here, we'll be right back," and we drove away. Evidently, I did not inherit my dad's love of driving or sense of adventure. I did not enjoy the ride. My long loose hair was flogging my face, but I didn't dare take a hand off the handlebar to straighten it. The Vespa felt wobbly, and I was afraid that if I didn't stand completely straight, I will topple it over. I was glad when Dad said we had gone far enough and turned around.

He brought us back to the Children's House just in time for lunch and promised to visit again soon to take us on another ride.

I'm not sure exactly when this happened, but it had to be around 1974-75. Was Dad on vacation from the hospital, or did he escape? Did he carry out his plan to earn money offering road service? Years later, when Dalia and I conducted our interviews, my uncle Yair told us about the origins of the Vespa. Anna, Saul's grandmother, gave him a gift, a television set, a rather expensive device back then. Dad traded it with someone for the Vespa. Saul's father, Ezra, was furious to the point that he tried to sabotage the vehicle, puncture the tire or something of the sorts.

Sinai

2016

"The next guy we are going to interview is Nathan. We're meeting him in his office at the Health Ministry. I expect it to be a short interview. He met our dad once and apparently has a good story about it," Dalia told Sasha. We were driving back to Jerusalem after our interview with Talia. In her hand Dalia still held the one postcard Talia managed to find.

"Okay," replied Sasha. "Other than the interview, what else do you want to film there?"

"With Nathan? Not much. Maybe some reaction shots of us. You know, the usual, listening, nodding, smiling. Some cutaways like his hand motions."

We parked at a parking garage and walked up hill the short distance to the address we had. I always found Jerusalem intimidating, like being in the presence of someone who takes herself very seriously. Draped over mountains, her streets are steep and tortuous, her buildings all made of heavy, cold, Jerusalem Stone. Going through the security screening of entering a government building, the metal detector, showing I.D. cards, stating the reason for our visit, and signing a guest book didn't make me feel more at ease.

We finally reached the office of Dr. Nathan Tal, director of the Ministry of Health. His assistant showed us into his office.

He welcomed us with a big, friendly smile, a man in his late sixties, his head shaved bald, wearing a dark blue button-down shirt.

Sasha and I examined the room, trying to decide on the best camera angle for the interview. The small office with its white walls and sparse decor didn't offer any great options. With Nathan's permission, we moved some chairs around and managed to find an angle that allowed proper distance of camera-subject and subject-background, with the window light coming from the side at a 45-degree angle.

While Sasha was setting up the camera, Nathan asked us if we had a photo of dad when he was young. Dalia found an old picture on her Facebook page of Dad with a woman we didn't know. Nathan said this is how he remembers dad but without the mustache.

When the camera was ready, Sasha asked Nathan's permission to powder his shaved head against shine, tested the microphone (one, two...one, two...) and we began.

Not sure what to expect, I asked Nathan to just tell us how he met Dad.

"I went with my three-year-old daughter and my wife on vacation to the Sinai peninsula." Nathan began, his eyes looking up to the left as if probing his memory. "I was an army doctor at Sayeret Matkal, and my commander let me borrow a military four-wheel-drive vehicle for that trip. I didn't have much experience driving off-road, but I was young and, like most young men, felt invincible," he continued with an apologetic smile.

"I heard about a place called Muyat Washwashe, a natural pool that filled up with rainwater and is a few kilometers from Nuweiba, accessible only by all-terrain vehicles. So, I decided to take my wife and daughter there. The car bounced on the sand and the rocks, and I felt like a hotshot. At some point, the path got much worse, with bigger boulders, and I decided to leave the vehicle and continue on foot. We walked another 40 minutes and got to the pool, which indeed was very nice. We swam in the cool water; I think it was May or June, a really hot day. When we'd had enough, we walked back to the car, and I realized one of the wheels was down on its rim; I had a flat. I tried to open the screws and couldn't. I tried again and again, and they didn't budge. I decided that there was no point in staying there any longer and I must get help. I lifted the little one on my shoulders, and we started walking back. It was a hot day, the sun was blazing hard, it was almost noon already, but we walked those few kilometers and finally made it to Nuweiba. I began asking around who could help me retrieve the army's vehicle. I had no experience in such situations, I had no idea what to do, I was at a loss. I was told there is no mechanic in the area, but then someone said there's this guy, he usually shows up around 4 in the afternoon on his moped, and he might be able to help. I had no other option, so we waited. It was still very hot, but at least we could sit in the shade.

"And indeed, just as I was told, at 4ish, a guy on a Vespa appears. I approached him and embarrassingly explained how my car got stuck on the way to Muyat Washwashe and people said that he might be able to help. Right away, he said, "Sure, no problem, I can help you, I can fix it, let's go." Nathan emphasizes the tale with a 'follow me' hand movement, and in his smile, I read a mix of nostalgia and wonder.

"I got on his moped, and we started driving. It wasn't really a road, more like a rocky trail, and he drove with no hesitation, pushing through like it was nothing to him. At some point, the sand and rocks made it impossible to keep riding, so he stopped, laid the moped on the ground, and we continued on foot, carrying the lug nuts opener and some oil or spray he had. We walked for another 40 minutes or so, and on the way, we talked. Turned out he was from kibbutz Ein Arava, and he told me all kinds of stories, fantastic stories about his time in Sinai, about women, colorful, funny tales about his adventures with tourists, I don't know. I was a young guy with lots of hormones, even though

I was there with my wife, and the stories really impressed me. We also realized we both served in the "Shaked" army unit, a few years apart, and it created another bond between us. Then we got to the vehicle and everything I tried and failed he did in minutes. Opened the nuts, removed, replaced, and we started to drive back. We got to his moped, he picked it up, and before we went back, I offered to pay him, and he requested such a ridiculously low amount that I was really embarrassed. That was it. Later, when I tidied up the car, I found some parts he left there, and I didn't know where I could mail them. I didn't have an address; I'm not sure I even knew his name. Maybe he gave me his first name; I don't remember.

The whole event stayed with me. I was in despair, and he saved me, and with such kindness and generosity. For years I had a vivid memory of that experience.

Years later, I worked as an internal medicine attending in a hospital, and every 2 or 3 months, we had new interns, and when it was quiet, we used to sit down and chat. One of my best interns was Ruth Keller, from Ein Arava. When she mentioned the kibbutz, it reminded me of the guy, and I told her about it. She listened very quietly, and when I finished, she said, "That sounds a lot like my brother, Saul." She told me all about him, about his mental illness, and how he used to run away from the psychiatric hospital on his Vespa when he was manic. All of a sudden, all the parts fit together.

Now many years later, I got a phone call from Ruth, now Professor Keller, an endocrinologist. We haven't been in touch or anything, and she tells me about her brother's death, and that you are filming a movie and asks me if I'd be willing to tell you the story of our meeting all those years ago."

Interesting, I thought. Here is a trained medical professional who had a close encounter with Dad, and it did not occur to him to question his sanity, probably because his conduct, even though somewhat eccentric, was not out of the range of accepted human behavior. In contrast, on the kibbutz, every time Dad raised his voice in public or became a bit chatty, someone went to talk to the family to say that Saul was again mentally unstable and maybe they should do something about it.

The kibbutz was a strong safety net for my dad, a place he could always return to. He had a small apartment and guaranteed minimum income, whether he was able to work or not. But whenever he became overactive, the net also limited his freedom to be himself, to act out in the way that is typical for hypomania (a low-grade manic state). Any time his behavior escalated, he quickly reached the boundaries of the net until he was trapped, subdued, tied, and delivered to the psychiatric hospital. Sometimes he managed to escape before they could catch him, finding freedom in the city, down south or abroad.

For several years, most of his escapes took him to the Sinai. At the time, a no-man's-land minimally developed peninsula, home to Bedouin tribes and bohemian Israelis, a place to sleep on the beach in tents or huts, known for its lax law enforcement and extraordinary coral reefs. Here, Dad could swim freely, showing his full colors, and no one looked at him funny or suggested that he belonged in an aquarium or institution.

Nathan, finishing his story, began to get up when Dalia interrupted him.

"Can I ask you something as a doctor and an official in the health department?"

He sat back, "Sure, go ahead."

"It's just that in the last few years of his life, we had a really hard time finding Dad proper psychiatric care...." she said, not exactly framing it as a question, but Nathan got the drift.

"First of all, I don't know if you're aware of it, but I'm the chairperson of the Binding and Restraint committee. You know that many mentally ill patients experience tying down and solitary confinement and the job of the committee is to set limits to that practice and make the care in psychiatric facilities as humane as possible. It's complicated because there's a shortage of personnel in psychiatric medicine, and such reforms usually require more human resources. Historically, psychiatric services in Israel were left behind compared to other areas of medicine. In the past, some people were kept in hospitals unnecessarily; it was common practice to stow them away, the mentally ill, not because they needed inpatient care or received any treatment, but to keep them confined and under control. Some of those places were just psychiatric warehouses." Nathan pauses as if he's just realized that this mini lecture which he has delivered many times before might be inappropriate or hurt us. When he sees us nodding in agreement, he continues in a gentler tone.

"You know…the thing is…the mentally ill, as individuals and as a group, are frail. They cannot advocate for themselves the way most of us can. That's where the family must step in, but even the families, as you pointed out, rely on existing services."

"And maybe some families prefer to stay out of it," I say. "I keep hearing stories of people who completely distanced themselves from a mentally ill parent. A friend of Dalia from work who came to the Shiva told us her father had PTSD, and she basically stayed away from him. She doesn't even know where he is now."

We talked a bit more; about whose job it is to promote the change (several government offices), what areas need the most work on (public opinion, family involvement in care, alternative care options within the community such as Halfway Houses or residential programs).

"Dalia, do you have any other questions?" I ask when the flow of the conversation ebbs.

"First of all, I'd like to thank you for that beautiful story. It's nice to hear stories not only about the disease but about the kind of person he was," she says.

"Yes, yes, that's why I remember that experience with such fondness. It wasn't only that he helped me when I was in serious trouble, leaving that army vehicle behind, completely helpless, but that he was so kind about it. He was truly glad to help."

"We have very little information about what he did whenever he disappeared," I joined in. "We know that he escaped from Mazra several times, and after weeks or months, I'm not sure, was captured and brought back, but no one knew what he did during those times; he didn't make contact because he didn't want to be found.

Forbidden Topics

1975

I knocked on the white painted door and heard Grandpa Ezra's shuffling feet inside. He opened the door wide and boomed, "Hello, hello, hello! Look who's here! Two princesses!"

Short and stocky, with ruffled graying hair, wearing a dark blue work shirt and worn sleepers, he ushered us in with grandiose gestures and began loading the small table in the living room with little plates piled up with strawberry-filled chocolate cubes, sliced Marzipan, homemade cookies, and other delicacies.

"Grandma Deborah will be here soon, she just went to the Dining Room to bring lunch. Are you hungry?"

He pulled up a chair and sat next to us, asking questions about school and our teachers, what are we learning in history, what books I've read lately. "Oh, I almost forgot," he said, with an exaggerated gesture of hitting his forehead with an open palm. "I got you something." In his heavy gait, he waddled to the other room. "How long can you stay?" he called back, still out of sight.

"Mom said she'll..." my sister started, and I shot her an angry look followed by a pinch to the arm. She stopped mid-sentence.

"We can stay until 5," I said, as Grandpa came back to the room, holding two books wrapped in brown paper.

I was nine, my sister was seven, and we were already burdened with family complexities. For years we knew that Grandpa Ezra did not speak to or mention our mother. Young as I was, I felt that it was my responsibility to keep Mom out of the conversation, afraid that if I slip and mention her, he'll get angry with me. It was a known fact that he could hold a grudge forever. Was I afraid to also become a target of his loathing?

I'm sure now that it was an unfounded fear. Our grandfather was strict in his morality and had a reputation for being difficult. Still, he was never anything but gentle and loving with us grandchildren. I'm sure if my sister or I had mentioned Mom, he would have ignored it or found a way to skirt around it. He was, after all, an exceptionally smart person and loved quibbling.

Later, I felt the same responsibility toward my dad. Always careful with my words, treading lightly on subjects that I thought might cause him embarrassment or discomfort.

At that moment, my grandmother walked in, holding a 3-tier stainless steel food carrier in one hand and a plastic basket with peaches in the other. She launched into a cheerful conversation, and the awkward moment was soon forgotten.

New Beginning, Again

October 1976

We lived on Kibbutz Assif, near Jerusalem, for three years while my stepfather completed his medical studies. In October 1976, a month after I began fifth grade, he took his final exam, and the family moved to the kibbutz he grew up in, Cfar Shibolim.

Dubi's parents, my step-grandparents, lived on Cfar Shibolim, so we visited often. I knew my way around; how to get from the gravel parking lot to the vast Dining Room complex, how to walk from there to the kibbutz museum where Grandpa Rudi worked, or across the water creek, gushing with water after the rain, smelling of decaying algae in the summer, to the grandparents' home. I knew how to get to the Children's Community, the kibbutz name for the elementary school, but I didn't really know any of the children.

Like last time we moved, Mom brought me to the Children's House on the first day to meet my new class and teacher. But here, the similarity ends.

On my first day on Assif, as soon as we walked into the class, the kids gathered around me, eager for my attention, each volunteering to show, explain, and help set up my things.

Here, on Cfar Shibolim, the only one eager to meet me was the teacher, Nurit. A small energetic woman, with wavy black hair greeted me warmly and showed me to the bedroom I was to share with 3 other kids. Two girls sitting on one of the beds raised their heads in a brief hi and went back to their whispering.

Nurit proceeded to show me around and introduce me to the children we passed in the hallway. They were mostly boys, and all showed about the same level of interest as the first girls. When we reached the showers, I paused, and Nurit, sensing my hesitation, said, "You can shower after everyone else if you prefer." I could have hugged her. What a relief. Did I not mention it before? In the kibbutz, everybody, boys and girls, showered together until the end of sixth grade. I was used to it, and it wasn't an issue before, with the kids I knew from second grade, but now, my body already showing the first signs of puberty, the idea of undressing in front of all those unfriendly kids was terrifying.

A blond, tall girl was reading a book on her bed, and Nurit called her over. She introduced her as Efrat and asked her to keep me company.

Efrat explained the situation; the class I joined had a large majority of males, 13 boys to 5 girls, a fact that the boys were incredibly proud of and hoped to maintain. The addition of a girl to the group was hence unwelcome. An "it's not you, it's your gender" situation.

So here I was, plucked from my comfortable environment and dropped into a new pack, on a new kibbutz, like a sheep removed from one farm and placed into a new herd. I kept circling but was not allowed in. My age group on the previous kibbutz was way more naive. There was no division between popular and unpopular kids, there was no "class king," or shunned children. Here there was a clear leader of the pack who everybody wanted to be friends with and who determined the ranking of the others. He ranked me untouchable, and most of the class followed his lead.

Like most childhood difficulties, it forced me to mature quickly.

Dalia, I believe, had an easier time. The third graders she joined had not yet developed the typical prickliness of pre-teens and embraced her with the natural naïveté of younger children. Having a sister across the lawn didn't help me though. Socializing with children of other classes, especially lower grades, was uncommon, so we rarely saw each other during the day. And at any rate, we weren't really close back then. She was my annoying little sister, not a peer.

My only ray of sunshine in Cfar Shibolim was Nurit, the homeroom teacher. She didn't just show me warmth; she highlighted my talents and encouraged me to develop my academic abilities. She recognized my strength in math and got me a subscription to a gifted children's mathematics worksheet that was published by the Israeli Institute of Technology. It was a thin, 4-page booklet, in small print, which contained challenging math and logic riddles. I devoured it, finishing the whole thing in a couple of days and then waiting impatiently for the next month's issue. If the previous move, in second grade, made me aware of my external peculiarities, this move revealed another layer, a core that would support me in the years to come; I discovered I was smart.

Social difficulties aside, at least the routine of life on a kibbutz was familiar. Although there were certain differences in schedule and customs, the basics were similar. The children lived, ate, showered, and slept in the Children's House, visited the parents for a few hours every afternoon, and took part in all other activities with their age group.

One custom that was new to me was the anticipated yet dreaded "Free Afternoon." Every Monday, instead of the afternoon nap time, the elementary school children were allowed to roam the kibbutz in small groups of friends they chose to hang out with.

It was the rare opportunity of non-structured free time that held the allure and the self-organizing small groups that were the source of anxiety for new, unpopular children like me. Many of those "Free Afternoon Gangs" had been together for months and were reluctant to invite newcomers. Others were led by a popular kid who welcomed or expelled members at a whim. The small number of children who did not make it into either would usually hang around the Children's House at the beginning of the afternoon, looking to see who they could pair up with.

It was a cloudy November afternoon, and looking around, I noticed Smadar, a girl of my age, pretending to be busy examining something on the ground on the other side of the yard. I decided to take a chance. I approached casually and looked over her shoulder.

"Hey, what's that?" I said, in the best matter of fact a voice I could muster.

Translation: "Are you with somebody? Are you looking for someone to hang out with?"

"It's a line of ants. Look how they are carrying that huge crumb," she said with a smile that meant, "Yes, I'm by myself; you are welcome to join me."

I sat next to her on the ground, and we watched the ants for a while. I picked a spiky seed pod off the weeds mixed in with the lawn and opened it, offering the seeds to the ants.

"What are you doing?" she asked.

"I'm opening the pods for them so they can get the seeds easier."

She picked up a pod and did the same.

"Do you want to take a walk?" she asked and sealed our partnership for the afternoon.

We walked towards the forested hill at the end of the kibbutz, talking about the school and the teachers. We passed other groups of children wandering around and ignored them. Same as they ignored us. "Is it true that Dubi isn't your real dad?" she asked. And I was surprised. I'd assumed that everybody on the kibbutz knew about my family's situation or at least that the class was briefed before my arrival.

"Yes, he is my stepdad."

"What happened to your real dad? Did he die?" Not an unusual question in war-plagued Israel.

"No, my parents are divorced."

We stooped to pick up wood sorrel flowers that grew on the side of the road. We called them "souries" due to their chewable lemon-sour stems.

"How come your dad never visits?" she asked, spitting out a chewed-up stem.

"He's in a mental hospital. He is not allowed to go out on visits now."

"Is he crazy?"

I launched into what was now a rehearsed explanation. I told her how my dad saw something horrible during an army operation, and it caused him to become sick with bipolar disorder. I explained how people who are Bipolar could sometimes be very depressed and sometimes act very happy, with no apparent reason, but in between behaved normal, looked, and talked like any regular parent. It was vital for me to separate my dad from the typical image of the mentally ill as it's portrayed in movies and sometimes seen in real life.

Smadar listened intently and asked some questions. As we headed back, we moved on to talk about other things. At the entrance to the Children's House, she said, "Don't worry, I won't tell anybody about your dad."

I said, "I don't mind if you tell anyone, there's nothing to be ashamed of, it's a disease like any other. It's nobody's fault." which was a statement I heard from my mom many times, and wholly subscribed to.

Letter to Abigail

September 1976

Abigail,

I just finished reading your letter for the fifth or sixth time, and I'm again happy to see that our friendship is mutual. I'm sending here a short journal I wrote. I'd like your opinion on the literary "talent" of the writer, using the pseudonym Samuel P.

Give my best to your family,

Warmly,

Saul.

Sunday 9/5/76

Yesterday I met Avi.

We are 83 patients in the secure ward, but Avi is the only one you could describe as "retarded."

He knows how to use the bathroom, and that's one of the reasons I agreed to take care of him, including changing his clothes if he wets himself at night.

For the last two days, I've been trying unsuccessfully to teach him my name (shortened to Sam instead of Samuel). I am not surprised since he doesn't even know his parents' names. He does remember the name of nurse Susan, the bully terrorizing all of us, although, under the hard cover, she hides a soft spot for the sicker patients. Still, Avi answers any inquiry about a name with the name Shoshana.

Mahmud is an old Bedouin, about 59 years old, who's been in here for almost 10 years (This morning, he told me a quarter of his life's story. I'll get back to it). He took care of Avi up until yesterday; slept in his room, fed him, changed his sheets and pajamas, everything I'm doing now.

This morning I woke up at 6 a.m. and saw Mahmud sleeping on a blanket without a mattress. (There are only 60 beds in the ward, and everybody else sleeps on mattresses in the hallway). Suddenly, the name "Nuweiba" entered my mind, but I hurried and pushed it back into the memory box and locked it well.

I checked Avi and he was dry, so I decided not to wake him up and see if he would stay dry until 7:15. As a result, I ended up changing his sheets and clothes and taking the mattress out to dry in the yard.

Avi had no visitors today, so I bought him sweets with my own money; I spent three Liras, a third of my daily allowance.

Then I got a big surprise; I gave him pretzel sticks, and he ate them happily, but then he saw a cookie in my hand and said "cookie." I couldn't believe my ears and asked him to repeat it, and he repeated it. It was the first time I heard him say a noun, not like a parrot repeating a word but as a result of knowing the word and using memory to retrieve it.

I have several ideas for activities to do with him, but there's no rush.

9/6/76

Avi and I face each other, and I still can't say for sure that there is a connection between us. Avi does what I tell him to do, but he never asks me for anything. Yesterday, he took advantage of my lack of attention and twice drank my extra strong cup of instant coffee. Luckily no staff member saw it.

This morning he woke up by himself at 6 o'clock and went to the bathroom. It is the first morning that he did not wet himself.

He is pretty finicky with food. He doesn't like soup or porridge. He just turns his head away and growls in refusal. Since I was never a proponent of force-feeding, I try to find out what he likes. He clearly prefers sweet and sour flavors.

This morning I tried to get him to play a board game. He played for 5 minutes (not necessarily following the rules), and I count it as a success.

Once I got him to say his father's name (Raffael?), but most of the time, he refers to everybody, including his parents and myself as Shoshana.

I noticed that he is getting a lot of medications. My guess is that he was violent before.

Avi often stands in the corner of the hallway with his finger on his temple. He also uses the same pose when lying in bed. When asked a direct question, he wrinkles his forehead with effort before giving up. I haven't heard him say a complete sentence yet.

Surprise! Just now, Avi said a full sentence, "I want juice." (Write about coffee-Avi).

Tuesday 9/7/76

This morning Avi got up and went to the bathroom by himself, and the bed remained dry. After that, he really doesn't require much care. Afterward, he managed to score a point in the Hat game, but his expression remained aloof without a hint of satisfaction. In general, it bothers me that he doesn't show any feelings. Maybe it will change? Hard to know.

Tonight I discovered that Avi can be crafty. He managed to find and eat the hidden box of candy his parents brought. He loves sweets. He also takes food out of the garbage cans and again today he drank my coffee when I wasn't looking.

It's been three days that I've been taking care of him, and he should have formed some bond with me, but he doesn't.

Sometimes he surprises me with a new word he says, but other times, he just stands in the corner of the room and hits the wall and himself repeatedly.

It's 10:45 pm, and he just got his sleeping pill. I hope he will wake up dry.

Letter to Daughters

December 1976

Mazra Mental Hospital, December 29, 1976

My beloved daughters,

Yesterday marked three years that I've been here (not deducting the time I ran away).

It's pretty depressing to spend so much time in such a repulsive place, but I have no choice.

I'm writing in pajamas since I'm not yet allowed to wear regular clothes, while sitting on a hot water bottle to relieve the swelling and pain caused by the injections I get. The way to freedom seems farther away than ever, and not getting replies to my letters doesn't help either.

I hope that after the Hanukah vacation, I will again receive letters from you and maybe a package with quality cigarettes that I miss so much.

Nitsan and Dalia , my beloved,

Write soon and frequently,

Kisses, Dad.

Visit

1977

The bus stopped on the shoulder and the automatic doors hissed open. My sister and I leaped off first and waited under the gray concrete and asbestos rain shelter. Grandma Deborah, wearing a simple floral cotton dress and sensible shoes, her wavy hair short and graying, descended heavily, one hand holding the railing, the other weighed down by a faded blue plastic basket bursting with various containers and boxes.

We crossed the road and started the long walk down the tree-lined entryway to the hospital. Grandma engaged us in her typical small talk, asking about school, friends, Mom and Dubi, and our younger half-sister and brother. We replied with long, funny stories, competing for her attention. A security guard came out of his booth, and when he was satisfied that we knew where we were going, he pushed a button to open the heavy blue gate and waved us in. Grandma led the way to "Open B," short for "Open Unit B," one of the hospital wards for low-risk patients.

At first sight, the grounds with their narrow sidewalks connecting low, one-story flat-roofed buildings, and the patchy lawns, strewn with benches and sitting areas, could be mistaken for a run-down college campus or a dilapidated, soon to be abandoned resort. But then you notice the bars on the windows, and the residents, many of them walking around in pajamas or robes, some shuffling their feet with the heaviness of the depressed or drugged, others bouncing in their walk with the animation of a young child trapped in an adult's body, and you realize this is no holiday destination.

Dad was waiting on the bench outside his unit, and when he noticed us, got up, and I saw with relief that he was wearing street clothes this time. The last time we were here, he was wearing hospital-issued pajama bottoms, a loose-fitting cotton thing with a fly that didn't quite close all the way. Throughout that entire visit, I struggled to keep my eyes away, horrified the pants might shift in a way that would expose his private parts.

He hugged us and took the heavy basket from his mom, and we all sat on the bench.

"It's so good to see you girls. I missed you so much!" he said, and again, I was relieved. Our last visit was shortly after he was brought back from one of his escapes. He was being treated with medicines that slurred his speech to the point that it was hard to understand. I had to keep asking him "what?" or pretend I understood and nod. He was also not inclined to talk much then, and I found myself laboring to keep the patter going, telling him about my friends and siblings and anything I could think of. I knew the medicines made him depressed, so I steered away from sad stories and concentrated on cheerful ones.

But today, he was in a good mood and happy to chat away.

"Mom, what did you bring?" he asked, motioning to the basket.

In reply, she made a space on the bench between her and my sister, laid on it a square embroidered cloth, and said, "Here, let's take some things out," while pulling from the basket an assortment of used fading plastic and tin containers.

Out came her famous Olive Bites and Puff Pastry savory sticks, a pomelo, already peeled and cut into bite size sections, and a chocolate bar. My dad reached over and took a pack of cigarettes out of the basket. He lit one with a plastic green lighter and then tucked the box and his lighter into his shirt pocket. He inhaled deeply and said, "These are sooo good, here all I can get are disgusting Ascots."

A woman came over and sat on the bench next to us, talking aloud to herself while motioning with her hands. I tried to ignore her, made an effort not to look in her direction, pretending there was nothing, no one unusual. My dad, however, got up, and hovering above her, barked, "This is a family visit, go sit somewhere else, leave us alone." She rose and left.

"Some of the crazy people here are so annoying," my dad said, without a hint of irony.

I guess I was lucky, in a sense, that my dad didn't look "crazy." He was fairly tall and slim with no external manifestations of his ailment. When he was depressed, a stranger might think he was tired or lost in thought. When he was manic, he seemed like a guy excited about an idea or event; no more abnormal than a fan whose team just scored an unlikely win. Only when he was heavily medicated did he seem sick, but that could be blamed on the doctors; it wasn't really him.

We ate the snacks and talked about our classmates, school, the Maccabi Tel-Aviv basketball team, and the upcoming Eurovision competition. Grandma gave updates from their kibbutz, who had a baby, who died.

At some point, my dad got up and said, "I almost forgot, I have something for you. Stay here. I'll be right back."

He came back a few minutes later, holding two small wooden boxes in his hand and accompanied by a male nurse in scrubs.

"Hey girls, this is Omar; he's a nurse on my ward; he's one of the nice ones. These are my girls," my dad beamed with pride.

"Wow, Saul, you have lovely girls. And you must be his mother?" Omar turned to Grandma and shook her hand. "It's very nice to meet you. And you girls. Your dad talks a lot about you."

When Omar left, Dad gave us each a handmade wooden box. "I made these in the woodworking shop in occupational therapy," he said. "You can use it for jewelry. Tsani, do you still have the necklace I brought you from Dahab?"

I nodded, although I wasn't entirely sure where it was.

When it was time to leave, we hugged him and promised to write and come back for a visit soon, and he said that hopefully, if he behaves well, he'll be allowed to come for visits on holidays.

Grandma gave him the remaining cigarettes and sweets, and we started the walk back to the bus station. Even though her basket was now empty, Grandma looked like she was carrying a much heavier weight than the weight she's arrived with.

Brave

1978

Dalia wiped the sweat off her forehead and felt herself smear some mush that stuck to her hand.

She and her fellow 5th grader, Dorit, were standing beside a large pile of wet bread leftovers, ladling portions into feeding bowls and chatting about nothing in particular, while other elementary school children delivered the food to the various fowl cages.

Like all elementary school children on the kibbutz, they worked for half an hour every morning before recess, rotating weekly between several chores. Some children cleaned the Children's House, some helped the caretaker fold laundry, and others, like Dalia that week, worked in the small petting zoo adjacent to the Children's Community.

An airplane from the neighboring air force base passed low overhead, filling the air with deafening vibrations and interrupting the girls' chatter. Two boys washing their hands at the sink raised their voices over the noise, and on the tail of it, Dalia could clearly hear her name and the words "crazies hospital."

She pretended nothing was amiss while scooping some feed into another bowl, straining to pick up more of the discussion.

A commotion at a nearby cage interrupted the conversation. Two ravenous geese attacked a food bowl, disregarding the boy still holding it, which caused him to drop it on the ground and run out screaming. Everyone rushed over, possibly to offer help but more likely to cheer or sneer.

When all the animals were fed and the cages cleaned, the children were dismissed. "Let's join the jump rope'" Dorit said when they approached the yard between the Children's Homes.

"I have a stomach ache; I'm going in," Dalia used an easy, irrefutable excuse. It was a common pretense among the 5th grader girls, later to be replaced by the sexier, more feminine headache.

Dalia locked herself in the bathroom, one of the only places she would be assured undisturbed privacy and sat on the closed lid to think.

Two days earlier, Dad visited the kibbutz for the first time in a while. Our family had moved to "Cfar Shibolim" two years prior, but he was hospitalized most of the time and didn't visit often. Some of Dalia's classmates knew that our parents were divorced, but as children often do, they accepted Dad's absence as a fact and didn't question it. A few others assumed Dubi was our father, even though she now, after being pestered by her older sister (yours truly), consistently called him by his first name.

The day Dad arrived, he was supposed to come directly to our parents' room after 4:30, when all the children went to their families until bedtime. But the bus, one of only three daily buses that reached the kibbutz, arrived just before 4 pm, so he asked directions from a passerby and arrived unexpectedly at Dalia's class.

Now in seventh grade, I was studying at the regional high school on another kibbutz and would arrive on the school bus later.

When Dalia first noticed Dad she was alarmed. In recent years she has seen him in different mood states, some unmistakably irregular, but she relaxed, realizing he seemed fine this time.

He lifted her up in the air and hugged her tightly while her surprised friends looked on. kibbutz children were not used to encounters with unfamiliar faces. He then sat her next to him on a bench and handed her a bag full of sweets.

"Here, share these with your friends," he said and signaled for the onlooking children to approach.

She took out a chocolate bar and handed a square to each of the kids who were overjoyed. Premium candy was a rare treat for kibbutz children and was usually reserved for special occasions.

At 4:30, they walked to our parents' room and spent a pleasant afternoon with everybody. In the evening, Dad walked her back to the Children's House to tuck her in and say goodnight. The kids who met him earlier greeted him with familiarity, and Dalia felt confident that he had made a good impression.

Now, sitting on the closed toilet seat, she wondered what went wrong. Some people in the kibbutz knew our dad from the army. Others may have been aware of Mom's previous marriage and the circumstances around the divorce. At any rate, one of those parents was either overheard discussing Dad's condition or shared the information with their child. The fact was that rumors of her crazy dad were apparently spreading. What was she to do?

It wasn't that she was ashamed of his condition, but she was afraid of children talking behind her back or mocking her.

What would Anne of Green Gables or Pollyanna do? Something brave and unexpected probably, but she couldn't think of anything.

For the rest of the day, she felt vulnerable. If she noticed children talking quietly, she was positive they talked about her. If someone sneered, it must have been about her crazy father.

In the afternoon Mom asked her if everything was okay. She considered telling her, but while trying to compose in her head what to say exactly, she found herself anticipating her reply which would likely be, "Pay no attention to those kids; the important thing is that you know your father has an illness that is nothing to be ashamed of, that it's not his fault, that he loves you and you love him..." Adult reasoning. Not very useful in 5th grade.

The following day, during homeroom class, it came to her.

They were sitting in a circle in the middle of the room. The tables that were usually arranged in a U were now pushed against the walls. Elisheva, the teacher, was making some final remarks about the educational game or exercise they had just concluded.

"We have a few more minutes," she said, "Does anyone have a question, comment, or issue they would like to talk about?"

Dalia raised her hand. "I want to say something."

"Go ahead."

"I... it's about my dad. My real dad, not Dubi. He is... he has a mental illness."

Encouraged by the teacher's sympathetic gaze and the silence in the class, she continued. "That's why he sometimes doesn't visit for a while. But he is okay now."

The class that was buzzing a minute ago with anticipation for breakfast fell silent.

"Dalia, that was very brave of you - telling the class about your dad. Is it okay if they ask questions? You don't have to answer if you don't want to."

Dalia shrugged, then murmured, "It's okay."

The room remained quiet. Embarrassed children examined their fingernails or the spots on the floor with rapt interest.

"It started during the war." She continued when no questions were asked. "Before I was born. He saw something awful, a tank running over a soldier, which gave him shell shock. And now he has a disease called Manic Depression. It means that sometimes he is really sad, and sometimes really happy, and sometimes he acts in a weird way and needs to go to the hospital. In between, he's regular."

"He doesn't look crazy," someone said in an attempt to reassure her.

Elisheva, noticing Dalia's discomfort, took over the conversation. "You know, many people have some form of mental illness, but they don't look or behave any differently than other people. They are not dangerous in any way. Mostly, they are suffering, and that's why they need to be at a hospital to get treatment and feel better."

She wrapped up the class, commended Dalia for sharing, and dismissed the children to go eat the breakfast that was waiting on the tables in the dining area.

For the rest of the day, Dalia felt special. Children smiled at her warmly, the teacher and caretaker paid her extra attention, and she sensed that she had done the right thing.

Two years later, at the beginning of 7th grade, Dalia and her classmates joined their peers from 3 other kibbutzes to study in the regional high school, nicknamed "The Institute". The kibbutz founders named the school "The Educational Institute," but now the word "Educational" remained only on official insignia and in formal addresses, and the rest of the time, it was called (aptly, according to students) The Institute.

The Institute sat on a sprawling campus, three miles from Cfar Shibolim. The students, besides attending lessons, also ate, worked, and slept there. Each age group was divided into two or three classes of approximately 20 children, and each class had its own stand-alone building. Daily buses transported the teens to their kibbutz if they wished to visit their parents in the afternoon.

The transition to The Institute was exciting for most. It symbolized another degree of independence from the parents and activities with the older kids. It also offered a fresh start for children who were not popular in their kibbutz; an opportunity to expand their social circle and meet like-minded friends.

At the same time, moving "up" to The Institute was dreaded by many. Children born in the kibbutz had minimal experience in meeting people they didn't already know well, and familiarity usually meant comfort. Everyone was used to physical imperfections or speech impediments, the tics, and the quirks of everyone else. Mixing up with new people threatened those with something to hide.

Dalia knew that rumors about her father would inevitably spread and decided to take action. The fact that the last time went so well was encouraging, but she was still somewhat concerned. She felt that the stakes were higher. At 13, kids tended to be more judgmental, and a girl's popularity more critical. What if one of the popular boys finds her dad's condition an easy target for ridicule?

She went to talk to Sara, her teacher, and told her that she would like to address the class in an upcoming homeroom lesson. Sara didn't ask what it was about but promised to give her the time.

The talk was surprisingly similar. Down to the "he really doesn't look crazy" remark. She again told the story about the tank in the war, explained in simple terms bipolar disorder, and was afterward wrapped in glowing affection.

In the afternoon, crossing the kibbutz from the bus drop-off to the family's home, Dalia decided to tell Mom about the talk. The fact that I wasn't on the bus to the kibbutz was encouraging. I was the family's cynic and would undoubtedly make some snarky remark that would dampen the experience if I was there.

As she walked the narrow path leading to the front door, Mom stepped out, startling her, and enveloped her with a tight hug. For a second, Dalia thought that something bad had happened. Our mom was never one to hug much.

"I'm so proud of you!" Mom exclaimed, her eyes glistening, "How mature of you!"

It took Dalia a moment to realize she was referring to the same class talk on her mind. Turns out that Sara approached her at lunchtime and told her, impressed and excited, about Dalia's address to her peers.

As for me, I heard about those daring public proclamations for the first time more than 30 years later, after my father's death, when I began badgering everyone for stories and memories.

It was Mom who brought it up.

Either by design or by accidental omission, at the time it happened, no one mentioned them to me, and rightly so. Teenage me would have snubbed the celebration of openness and honesty, declaring that the mere act of the announcement is an admission of a shameful secret.

For me, things were different. It wasn't that I didn't care about my social status. I did. Immensely. But I worried about other things. Like my acne situation, my height and weight, and my monthly period that began early and was a challenge to hide from my classmates in our shared living space.

However, I was never ashamed of Dad's illness and mostly didn't care who knew or talked about it. And the fact that he had a normative appearance, that "he didn't look crazy," helped.

As an adult and a mother, I do think that Dalia's actions were commendable. Not only for discussing Dad's condition but generally for being proactive about an issue and taking steps to solve it. As a writer and filmmaker tackling the subject of mental health, I also now understand that society is still lightyears away from seeing it the way we did in fifth grade.

Jail

March 6, 1979

My beloved daughter,

Let me begin with an apology for my handwriting (that isn't great even under ideal conditions). It's just that at the place I'm currently staying, there is no desk, not even a single chair, and there is no possibility of leaving to find those elsewhere. But enough with the hints. I am currently in the Be'er Sheva jail, on the way from Ophira to Mazra. I'm writing lying down while leaning on my right elbow.

The room here is 21x12 feet and has 6 bunk beds and 12 inhabitants. An interesting assortment of characters of all ages and criminal occupations.

Unfortunately, I am used to that kind of company. If it was up to me, I wouldn't choose to spend more than a couple of hours with this crowd, but I can see the benefits in it, especially the opportunity to observe and learn about human nature and escape boredom.

The conditions here are not bad at all. The bathrooms are clean, there is hot water in the shower, the food is served on tables and is reasonable in quality and quantity.

If I sound optimistic, it is for a simple reason- the vast improvement in my situation compared to the last 10 days.

Let me start from the beginning, Saturday, February 17 (Although I suspect that this will turn into a much longer letter, probably the longest I've ever written you. It will detail the history of my illness since March of 1968). I took a car and drove to Jerusalem and Tel Aviv for 2 days. From there, I went to Dahab, a Bedouin village next to a nudist (people who walk around naked) beach. After a couple of days, I arranged for a group of 5 tourists to go on a trip in return for sharing the gas expenses (it's a great car with unbelievable performance off-road, large, strong engine that eats a lot of gas, and I was short on cash).

We toured the central plains of Sinai for 3 days, visited Santa Katarina, and continued to the western coast, the Gulf of Suez, and Ras Muhammad. Ras Muhammad has the most beautiful underwater landscape in the world with numerous types of stunning colorful fish swimming within the exquisite coral reef. It was an incredible experience. Together with the opportunity to speak English that I enjoy so much and the company of the tourists, it was well worth it!!!

On Friday morning (February 23), I was stopped by the Ophira police, and it didn't take them too long to figure out my circumstances. They arrested me. However, on the way to Eilat (I was riding in the police car, and someone else followed with my car), we stopped in Neviot for a break. I took advantage of the policemen's momentary lack of attention, took my car and escaped. I drove back to Santa Katarina and then to the West. The next day, after a TV movie-style car chase, I was arrested again and delivered to the Eilat police station where I spent the worst 10 days of my life. If the conditions of the Eilat jail are not the worst in the country, they must be second or third. I will not go into details, but I'll just say that the company was especially unpleasant, the handling of the inmates unnecessarily cruel (including unprovoked beatings), the food vile, and only the more or less regular supply of cigarettes kept me going.

Tsani,

It's almost "lights out" time here (10:30) at the Be'er Sheva jail, so I've decided not to burden you with more details and to end the letter here. I will write to you from the hospital and tell you more. It's time for you to know all and everything.

I have plenty of time here for thoughts and missing the people I love. I miss you with all my heart. I'm glad we recently spent 2 good evenings together.

Kisses and bye, Dad.

<u>March 7</u>

Good morning Tsani, my dear daughter,

I actually finished writing this letter last night, but since I have unlimited paper and ink in my Parker pen and it flows on demand, I will add a few more words, not about my "adventures" but from heart to heart.

I miss you a lot, Tsani, and more so in difficult times. I never liked sentimental gushing, but I want you to know that I have no one other than you and Dalia.

My relations with my parents and Yair and Ruth are based on help and support but not on deep feelings, and my latest prank will probably not help. This is why I enjoyed our basketball evenings together- just us- so much.

Did you receive the "Mikron 3" necklace I sent you?

Tsani, write to me at "Mazra" and come visit as often as you can- at your age, you are allowed to enter the secured ward for a visit. I will ask Yair to drive you.

All my love and I hope that you understand and forgive,

Kisses and bye,

Dad.

* * *

Dad never got around to "detailing the history of his illness since March of 1968," as promised, at least not in any of the letters I found. But he obviously wanted me to know.

Recording

Summer 1979

"When you're done with the coffee I'd like to have a private word with you for a minute." My mom said to my dad, in an apologetic tone, and my ears jumped up like a Doberman puppy hearing the mailman's footsteps.

My dad was on leave without permission (his term) for a couple of weeks from the mental hospital and came to visit us in Cfar Shibolim for the afternoon. As usual, my mom, stepdad and younger siblings greeted him warmly and there was never any tension. So, when my mom asked for a "private word" I was surprised, curious, and a bit alarmed.

We were sitting in the small kitchen in my parents' one bedroom apartment. On the table was spread an assortment of the usual offerings my dad brought; specialty pickles from the kibbutz factory where he worked when he wasn't in the hospital, candy he purchased on the way at the central bus station and a booklet of jokes, caricatures, and crossword puzzles he always bought for the ride and then left for me.

Dad's coffee was still hot and he was sipping it slowly so I had a minute to scheme. I had to know what that "private word" was all about. I got up from the kitchen table, and my sister followed me. We went to the bedroom, the only real room in the apartment and the only place where they could talk privately. It was a small room, mostly taken up by a double bed with a simple wooden frame. There were shelves loaded with books on the walls all around, and a small brown laminated desk. On the desk was the tape recorder I was aiming for. There was no time to waste. I saw that there was a cassette inside so I pressed "record," covered it with a pile of newspapers that were next to it and we went back to the kitchen.

When they saw us, they stopped talking.

"Nits, I want to talk to your dad for a second, do you mind going to the other room?" my mom said.

"But we want to play here. Maybe you can talk in the bedroom?" I said innocently.

They got up and went to continue the conversation in the room as I'd suggested.

When they were done talking, and came back to the kitchen, I waited a little and then found an excuse to go to the bedroom. I turned off the recorder and took out the cassette. To my horror I realized that we recorded on my half-sister's favorite program, a recording of the musical "Topelle" she was listening to practically every day. I quickly scanned the small room for a reliable hiding place and decided that the record cabinet was a good choice. It was a low cabinet, just slightly deeper and taller than the dimensions of a standard record. The records were arranged standing up with a few wooden dividers to support them. I pulled out a handful of records, placed the cassette all the way at the back and arranged them as they were. I closed the cabinet door and returned to the kitchen to join the rest of the family.

The next day, when my parents were at work, my sister and I snuck to the house to listen to the recording.

I retrieved the cassette from the records cabinet, placed it in the recorder and pressed "play."

"As I was saying," my mom's tone sounded somewhat apologetic," I don't know who, but one of the parents in Nitsan's class complained about the joke booklets she brings. There are some, how to say it, dirty jokes?"

So, this is what it was all about, I thought, those "sex" jokes? How naive do those parents think we are at 13? There was nothing there that we haven't seen or heard elsewhere.

My dad promptly apologized and promised not to bring those joke booklets again. We listened to the rest of the conversation and the only other part of interest was when my dad asked if we might be listening in on them or recording them and my mom dismissed the idea. It's funny how dad, who saw us so infrequently, still knew me so well. Or maybe it was just something that he would do? We put the cassette back in the hiding place and would have forgotten all about it if it wasn't for our little sister who asked to listen to her favorite musical and the recording was nowhere to be found.

Many years later, when we came clean, we offered to buy her the record but she was no longer interested.

Regrets

2015

Grandma Deborah was born in 1922 in Vienna (my father was born in '44, and I was born in '66. My dad, obsessed with dates and numbers, naturally expected me to have my first child in '88. As much as I appreciated the beauty of the numerical pattern, I didn't have a baby then). She was the fourth child to an educated Jewish family.

Her father was a high school teacher (Professor in German), and her mom "Frau Professor," meaning the wife of a professor (women professionals were extremely rare back then).

The rise of the Nazi regime in Germany and Austria prompted the family to leave their home and make their way to Palestine, where the Zionist movement was hoping to establish a country for the Jewish people. The parents built their home in Jerusalem while their 5 children joined the settlers movement.

Deborah, 16 years old when she first arrived, remembers a ride on a truck full of supplies and the instruction to keep their heads low for fear of being shot at by the Arab villagers.

She was sent to kibbutz Tel-Yossef and there met the Polish immigrant Ezra Leventhal. They later got married and had 4 children, Saul, Yair, Ruth, and Uri, who suffered oxygen deprivation at birth and was severely developmentally impaired.

As a child, I remember Grandma Deborah as a no-nonsense, industrious woman. While Ezra was the idealist, always touting kibbutz doctrine, a lover of Yiddish literature, who always welcomed us with a generous spread of chocolates and other delicacies, she was the practical one, who planned our visits and returns, who (at least as far as I knew) took care of Dad's needs on the kibbutz.

Grandpa Ezra was the one who didn't talk to, about, or even acknowledge our mom's existence after her divorce from Dad. He was also the one who insisted on keeping Uri on the kibbutz, despite the growing difficulty of caring for him.

Grandma remained on good terms with my mom and Dubi, visited us occasionally, and was the one to phone with news about Dad.

When I began my research into Dad's life, I imagined Deborah would be the one who could fill in the gaps in the story and illuminate details of events that happened when we were young. Even at 93, she had better clarity of mind and memory than many people half her age.

Like with other members of my dad's family, I wasn't completely comfortable asking. In my head, I anticipated the "what is it good for" response. Knowing my grandma was agreeable and always aiming to please, I expected the reproach would not be voiced, but I could still hear it nice and clear.

So, I asked, and she said yes, and in June, when I came to Israel for the headstone unveiling, I scheduled an interview with her and made sure Dalia would accompany me for moral support.

I knocked on the off-white wooden door, and Grandma answered with her soft Austrian accent, "Yes, yes, come in, come in."

I walked into the familiar one-bedroom apartment. Deborah waited for me, wearing a cotton floral dress (there must be someone somewhere making those shapeless dresses, especially for the kibbutz's elderly members. I've never seen them sold anywhere). Her hair, almost entirely white, in a short, practical cut and her creased face free of make-up.

She used to be a tall woman, at least in my memory, but she

has shrunk over the years. Because I only see her now once or twice a year, I notice it every time.

"That's a lot of equipment," she commented with a chuckle as I unloaded the tripod bag and camera off my shoulder and placed them on the floor. Not really, I thought, glad I decided to film by myself with a smaller camera.

I looked around the living room, which also served as her bedroom, trying to decide the best angle to shoot.

The entire space was about 14x20 feet. A twin-sized bed and a tall wooden wardrobe stood against one wall. Across the room was a TV on a short stand and a low bookshelf with a radio, a few children's books, and some photos. The dead men of the family; Grandpa Ezra, Uri in his wheelchair, and my dad, were all watching me out of simple frames, wondering why the heck I was bothering Grandma with this nonsense.

Dalia texted she was running late, so I decided to start on my own.

"So what we really want is... We feel there are many things about Dad we never asked him, or anybody else, and all of a sudden he...." I opened, using "we" to distribute the blame. Deborah nodded.

"So, how do you remember him as a boy with his siblings and his classmates?" I asked.

"I remember one thing," she chuckled, "When Ruth was in kindergarten, she cried a lot, and Saul, his class was just across the road, in the Dutch Houses, would go over and soothe her."

"He had friends in his class," she continued, "Shlomo and Abigail, and what was her name... Segal's daughter... Abigail always told me how smart he was; she said he was practically a genius."

"How about Yair? Were they close?"

"No, I don't think so. He had a stronger connection to Ruth when they were young."

"And Uri?" I asked.

"They took care of him. In the beginning, it wasn't hard, but it got harder with time. I think we made many mistakes with Saul because we were so busy with Uri, but well…" Again, the familiar little chuckle, this time accompanied by a slight shrug.

"What do you mean by mistakes?"

"Maybe we should have consulted earlier when his troubles began. He was hospitalized a few times but then was fine again."

"Were there any signs something was wrong before Karameh?"

"I don't know… at the end of senior year, he stole cars a few times and went on joy rides, but I don't think it had anything to do with it."

As a child growing up in the Children's House, I didn't consider the arrangement too unusual, and definitely not abusive or neglectful. Of course, I knew almost all the children in the world lived and slept in their parents' homes, but I was used to it, and anyway, most of the kids I knew lived just like me.

Over the years, numerous people raised in a kibbutz came out (in books, interviews, and lawsuits) with accusations of maltreatment. Some of them regarding specific, unusual occurrences, but many addressed the system as I knew and accepted it.

In many cases, the accusations were pointed toward the accuser's parents, who chose to live on the kibbutz and subject their child to the Communal Sleeping (as it was sometimes referred to) System.

A few years ago, Oryan Chaplin, a former kibbutz member, published the book "Four Hours a Day" and took the conversation in a new direction. She interviewed kibbutz mothers. Despite the fact that those mothers chose to live on the kibbutz (or at least were part of that decision), many, especially those who grew up in a traditional household, talked about feelings of guilt and regret.

What was it like for Deborah, who grew up in a warm home

with her parents and 4 siblings, to leave her own children in the Children's House? How did she feel when her older son was the one who heard his sister crying and went to console her while she was somewhere else? Or when her son was stealing kibbutz cars, and she was only remotely aware of it?

"So it all began in Karameh?"

"Yes, you know, that thing with the tank. And Ginath was there and took him to Talbiya. Then he was fine for a while, but it started again. There isn't a mental hospital in Israel he hasn't stayed in."

Deborah paused, her eyes cast down, her gaze distant, and I waited.

"There was this one time when he took you to Jerusalem," she raised her eyes, "Or I took you to visit him in the hospital, and he ran away, and you cried, and I had to take you back to Ein Arava...."

"Wait," I interrupted. This story was new to me. "You and I went together to Jerusalem?"

"Yes, to visit him, I think or... No, that was a different time when he took you from the kibbutz, and they tried to chase him, and you ended up at my mom's house."

She went on to recount other goods he took without permission during those years, such as kibbutz-property furniture, checks from his grandmother, and the army weapon from his roommate.

"With this weapon thing, what happened?" It was a story I was trying to understand better.

"There was a trial; I was at the court," she replied, "but they recognized he was sick and sent him to Mazra. He was there for several years, three or four."

"The court sentenced him for a certain duration?" I asked.

"No, he was depressed for a long time."

"But he also ran away on a few occasions."

By the letters he sent from Mazra, and the fact that he repeatedly escaped, I can confidently say that he wasn't continuously depressed. I wondered to what extent was he hospitalized for care, or was it also a form of punishment? Dalia and I made several attempts to obtain the medical records but failed. It was too long ago; files from those years are kept in some off-site archive, and customer service in those places is not a priority.

There was a quick knock on the door, and Dalia entered, apologizing for being late.

"How's it going?" she asked Grandma after taking a seat next to me.

"We were just talking about those years in Mazra." Deborah filled her in.

"How long was he there?" Dalia asked.

Grandma thought for a minute, "Well, he must have entered in 74 after the Yom Kippur War, and I think he was there until 1980. Other than the times he ran away. At some point, they arranged for him to study carpentry at a nearby trade school. I still have that sewing box he made there," she pointed to a yellow, 3-tier sewing organizer on the shelf behind me.

"He made that?" I was surprised. It's always been on that shelf, but I never gave it any thought.

"After Mazra he had some stable years, good years," Grandma seemed to perk up talking about that time.

"He worked at the pickle factory, first on the labeling machines and later on the forklift. When he was well, he was a hard worker, very reliable...."

Whoop-de-doo, I thought to myself. My genius dad did a great job pasting labels on food cans.

Dalia must have read my mind because she asked, "How come he never studied anything real? Could he?" She meant; would the kibbutz have allowed it? Higher education studies in the kibbutz were not a given. Most kibbutz members did not study beyond high school. The ones who did, had to get the kibbutz's permission and funding, and those were reserved for occupations needed in the kibbutz, like teachers or nurses. My uncle Yair studied food technology because the kibbutz needed it for the pickle factory.

"I don't know," Deborah said. "After he ran away from the kibbutz a few times, he wasn't considered a member anymore. Although they still made sure he had what he needed, more or less."

"He was fairly lonely on the kibbutz, wasn't he?" More of an observation than a question.

"Yes. In the early years of his illness, he always had a contact person in the kibbutz he could talk to or ask if he needed anything, but later it was mostly the family."

"I had the feeling Yair had a hard time with it; that it embarrassed him whenever Dad was acting out," I said.

"Maybe," she replied. "He was somewhat reluctant, but he helped him when he needed it."

"So, for several years, you had to take care of two sons with special needs," Dalia observed.

"Yes, I told Nitsan before you came that maybe it got in the way of taking care of Saul. We had to be with Uri all the time. Maybe we missed something. I don't know."

Regret is an unusual emotion. Unlike the experience of anger or jealousy, it is derived from a place of rumination, of examining possible other scenarios. At the same time, regret is more than a simple appraisal or judgment; it is typically loaded with feeling and therefore qualifies as a true emotion.

Some evidence suggests there is a temporal pattern to the experience of regret; that actions, or errors of commission, generate more regret in the short term, while inactions, or errors of omission, produce more regret in the long run.

How often, over the last 50 or so years, has Deborah lain awake at night, wondering if there was something else she could have done, if a different course of action, an earlier intervention, could have resulted in a better outcome? If not a completely disease-free life, at least a less solitary one?

"But after Mazra, he had several good years," she repeated as if swatting away a bothersome thought. "He met Rachel and she came to live on the kibbutz with Noam. I think he was in second grade. We had good relations with him. He used to come to our room often, and I used to take him to his music lessons and to the swimming pool."

Rachel, my dad's one long-term girlfriend, was a small quiet woman with very short dark hair and glasses. She was always pleasant with Dalia and me, but we didn't have a close relationship with her or her son. She and my dad met on an organized "singles" hike, I think. She moved to the kibbutz in the early 80s and stayed until 1994 or '95. At first, they lived together in his apartment, but she had a low tolerance for his chain-smoking, and he had a low tolerance for her active young child, so she got a separate apartment. She was a pleasant person and a reliable worker, a quality that was appreciated by kibbutz members.

When her son graduated high school, she moved back to Tel Aviv. Dad and Rachel still saw each other on weekends for a few years, but I'm not sure precisely until when.

"How was his relationship with Ezra?" Dalia asked.

"Well...Ezra...He took it hard; he got outraged whenever Saul did those...you know... stealing and stuff. But he still tried to help pull strings so the kibbutz would show leniency. When Saul was in Mazra, he took 2 buses every Saturday to visit him and bring him bananas. I also went sometimes. I remember sitting with him on the bench outside for an hour in silence. It was tough."

"Have you ever had any real personal conversations with him about the disease?" Dalia again.

"No, I don't think so. I tried a couple of times, and he didn't want to talk. I mean, I'm not a big talker, and he wasn't either. Not heart-to-heart talks."

"I still feel there's so much I don't know about him, about the earlier years," I said.

"It's hard to remember," Deborah replied.

"Who else on the kibbutz was in touch with him, like his contact person?"

"Yes, there were a few, but they've all passed already. They all made an effort with him, but he had a falling out with all of them. I guess they asked things of him he wouldn't do? But they all tried hard."

"I think when he was manic, everybody was afraid to confront him," I said.

"Yes." Deborah nodded.

"And he did hold a grudge against anyone involved in stopping him or committing him, including Ruth and Yair. Probably also people from the kibbutz." I said.

"Yes, that was usually true," Dalia joined in, "Us also, at least I, hesitated every time he was manic, afraid if I got involved he would be upset with me after. But I also knew he would always forgive us."

I checked the time. It was almost 1:00 - time for grandma to eat lunch and for us to walk over to Yair's house for another interview. We said goodbye and see you soon. We will be back tomorrow for the headstone unveiling ceremony.

Telephone

1990

The phone kept ringing inside the empty nurse's station. An elderly man was slumped in a plastic chair, his eyes glazed over, chanting "Telephone... Telephone..." in a monotone voice, pausing for a few seconds between words. Both him and the phone went unanswered.

My sister tried to peek into the booth, looking for someone to ask, while I was scanning the large room full of men, to see if I can spot our dad. A fog of cigarette smoke hung above a sea of light blue pajamas, and together with the hushed murmurs of the patients, a medicated illusion of tranquility was created.

Two days ago, my dad called me in the evening.

After the usual hellos, he told me about his idea. He was going to organize a reunion of his army unit. He'd already made a list of invitees, and he began to recount it for me. He went on about his plans, but I already knew where it was going. When he finally hung up, I called my sister.

"Dal, do you have a minute? Can you call Dad? Tell me what you think."

I didn't have to elaborate. She knew what I was asking. We've been through this before.

She called me back ten minutes later.

"Yup, He's definitely 'going up.'"

"What should we do?" I asked.

"I don't mind calling Grandma, but I'm sure they noticed it already. They'll probably hospitalize him soon."

Yesterday afternoon I came home from the university to find Dad at my apartment, crouched on the floor in front of my TV set connecting wires. I was an undergraduate student at Tel-Aviv University, and I was living with my boyfriend, Oded, in a Tel-Aviv apartment owned by Dad's girlfriend, who currently lived with him on the kibbutz. He had a key and let himself in, bearing extravagant gifts: a video cassette player and a large selection of cassettes. He was obviously manic.

I made coffee, and we sat down to drink it with some cookies. He talked nonstop, telling me about some new grand plan while eating the cookies one after the other. I tried to pretend what he was saying made sense, to go along with his enthusiasm. I feared that if I showed skepticism, I'd upset him or embarrass him.

Spending time with him in this state was exhausting, so when he asked me to drive him downtown, I was relieved. It was getting dark, and my dad, who usually knew the city very well, was getting confused, erroneously naming landmarks and streets. I knew he wasn't well, but I didn't challenge him. The job of confronting him, restraining, forcing hospitalizations, always fell on his parents and the kibbutz. Over the years, on many occasions, I heard him talk about those incidents as a betrayal and as a result, his relationship with his family was strained. Anything I would do to cut his evening plans short is sure to be viewed by him as treason.

After dropping him off, I went home and called my grandma. I told her he was manic again (she wasn't surprised) and where I dropped him off.

Earlier today, my grandmother called to say Dad was arrested in Tel Aviv the night before and was now under observation at the Abarbanel mental hospital. She didn't have more details. I called my sister, and we agreed I'd pick her up after work to go see him. Oded offered to come with us.

"Are you sure" I asked. Oded and I have been together for 3 years, and I knew he liked my dad, but he never saw him in an unstable mental state. Besides, I've been visiting mental hospitals all my life, and it's not an easy experience. He said he was sure, but I was still hesitant. Eventually, we agreed he'd drive us but wait for us outside. Before we left, he grabbed an extra pack of cigarettes to bring to my dad.

"I guess it was to be expected," I said as soon as my sister got into the car.

"Yup. I don't think anybody from the kibbutz even tried to find him."

I spotted Dad across the room, looking like he aged 10 years since I last saw him. What yesterday was a helium-filled balloon bouncing full of energy was now a small piece of damp rag as Piglet would put it. We walked over to him; he was sitting with his head down, food crumbs in his cigarette-stained beard.

As we approached, he looked up in recognition. With his chin, he pointed toward a pile of plastic chairs in the corner. He placed a hand on his chest and coughed, wincing.

"The police, they broke my rib," he mumbled in a Haldol-induced slur.

"What? Why?" I asked incredulously.

"I tried to take the minibar out of the hotel room, so they called the police."

"The drinks?" my father was never a drinker.

"No, the little fridge."

And of course, he resisted arrest.

We stayed for a little while. He didn't talk much, so we did our best to keep the conversation going. Eventually, he said he was tired and wanted to lie down, and we got up to leave.

On the way out, the phone was still ringing, and Telephone Guy was still chanting.

We walked to the car in a somber mood until I started imitating

"Telephone...Telephone," and we both burst out laughing. I find that a good laugh, much like a good cry, is the best remedy for tension.

For years after, my sister and I would imitate that chant and chuckle. Our own private "cuckoo's nest" moment.

I'm not sure if I understood it that day, but this was the event that transformed Dalia and me from mere concerned daughters to caregivers. That day I understood we can no longer expect other family members to take responsibility for our father when he's ill, and we need to step up. Luckily, the next major event was still 6 years ahead.

Geneva

November 1996

I placed the kitten back in her cage and marked an x in the appropriate square on her chart, indicating I'd completed the 8 p.m. treatments.

I was ready to grab another clipboard when the intercom's loudspeaker thundered: "Student Nitsan Tal, Student Nitsan Tal, a phone call on line 3." I picked up the phone.

"Hello?"

"Nits, it's me. Are you busy? Can you talk?" asked my sister, not bothering with small talk. It was clear that if she called me at the school, she had something important to discuss.

"I can talk, but not for long. We're in the middle of evening treatments."

It was my first month as a 4th-year veterinary student, my first night rotation in the Small Animal Internal Medicine Unit; I didn't want to make a bad impression.

"OK, I'll try to be brief. Grandma Deborah just called me. Abba flew to Europe. Nobody knows where he is."

"What?"

"Yup. That's a new one. Apparently, this morning, around 10 am, he ran into a member of the kibbutz at Ben-Gurion Airport. He told that person he was flying to Europe and gave him the keys to the kibbutz car he'd parked in the parking lot. That person called Deborah to tell her about it, but they didn't really know what to do. A couple of hours ago he called Rachel and told her he'd purchased a ticket on the first flight he could find and is now in Europe. He wouldn't tell her what country he was in. He said he was fine and not to worry."

"Shit. Sure he's fine." I said sarcastically.

At that moment, the intern in charge walked in and looked at me questioning.

"I'm sorry, I have a bit of a family situation; I'll finish the treatments soon," I said. She must have seen something in my expression because she said:

"Do you want to go talk in the interns' office? There's nobody there. I'll finish the treatments."

Relieved, I put my sister on hold and went to pick up in the other room.

"So how are they planning to find him?" I asked when I got back on the line, by "they" referring to my grandma and the kibbutz. Somehow, despite prior evidence to the contrary, I still expected them to take charge.

"I don't know. From talking to Deborah, it seems like they're not going to do anything."

"Are you serious?"

"Yes. Deborah sounded so tired on the phone. Like she can't deal with it. Look, she's 74, she doesn't have the energy for it. I also don't think she knows what to do."

"And someone from the kibbutz?"

"I don't think anybody there will help either."

"OK. Let's think about what we can do. I really can't do much tonight; I need to go back to work. Do you think you could call the airport or airlines and see if they can tell us if he was on a flight?"

"Okay, let me try. I'll call you back."

As I hung up, the intern walked in.

"Are you alright?" She asked.

She was someone I was quite intimidated by. Definitely not someone I expected to ever have a "heart to heart" with. But that evening, I told her my life's story.

Around 11 p.m., my sister called back. She was unable to get any information from the airlines due to privacy rules and whatnot. We agreed we'd talk in the morning and think about what to do next.

In the morning, we devised the only plan we could think of. My sister prepared a letter explaining my father's condition, and as much as we knew about his situation. She included the best photo she could find at home. I don't remember how she got the fax numbers of all the Israeli consulates in Europe during this pre-Google era (how did we do anything back then?) but she did and also got permission to use her office fax for that purpose.

Then we waited. Honestly, I didn't think it would work. I thought it more likely that he'd run out of money or get in trouble and eventually call us. I was extremely concerned he may get into an unfortunate encounter with police in a language he doesn't speak.

To our surprise, four days later, my sister got a call from the consulate in Geneva. Someone from a hotel contacted them to say that an Israeli citizen named Saul Lavie left his room without paying. They had his passport, what should they do with it? The consulate person promised to contact the local police and ask their help to find him.

The next day they had him. They said he was fine and cooperating. They would arrange for him to get on a return flight to Israel, but the airline required that someone from the family accompany him. I said I'd go. My passport was up-to-date, and I was fairly confident that the school would give me a couple of days off for a family emergency. There was also the issue of money. He owed about 1000 Swiss Francs to the hotel. As we were trying to figure things out, the consulate contacted us again and said he seemed to be acting reasonably, and they would put him on a flight the next day.

I was on night shift again, so Oded went to pick him up from the airport and drove him to Rachel's apartment in Tel Aviv. He called me when he got home and said that Dad seemed okay. He was a bit skinnier and had visible bruises on his face, but otherwise fine.

That was the first time that I knew that my dad had recovered from a manic episode without medical intervention with tranquilizers.

I called him in the morning.

"Dad?"

"Tsani!" He was happy to hear me.

"Dad, are you OK? What happened?"

"Ah, I was stupid. I went to visit Rachel for the weekend, and I forgot to bring my medications, so I started getting 'high.'"

"Where have you been? What did you do?"

"I flew to Geneva, it was the first flight I could get. I stayed in a hotel for a couple of days, but then I ran out of money. They had my passport. I couldn't get it back without paying, so I left it there."

"Then what?"

"I slept in a park, on a bench. Switzerland is so nice and clean."

"Oy. Were you okay? Weren't you cold?"

"A bit. Mainly I was hungry. But then they came looking for me. The consulate, they knew who I was, I think someone from the kibbutz sent a fax with my picture." I did not correct him.

"You were lucky! We were very worried about you."

"I know, I'm sorry. But I'm fine now."

Many years passed before I told him the truth about our involvement. Although I accepted the fact my sister and I were now responsible for him, I wasn't ready to let him in on it. Like most fathers, for him, we were still his little girls. We didn't want to shatter the illusion, to further chip away at his dignity, his already fragile self-esteem. Most people, I imagine, go through this process gradually as their parents age; first helping them with little things, then more, until at some point, the child-parent roles are reversed completely. For my dad, I always feared it would be abrupt, and we did our best to postpone that day.

Jungle Gym

2004

My mom sighs with relief as she brushes away some pine needles from the bench and takes a seat next to me. For the last 20 minutes, she's been safeguarding my son on the rusty jungle gym while I was watching from afar. My pleas for her to sit down, pointing out that he climbs this kind of equipment regularly, fell on ears plugged by concern.

Now he finally descended the treacherous heights to ride a tame wooden horse, and she allowed herself to relax.

"He's not afraid of anything, is he?" she says, her grandma pride picking through her mock exasperation.

"No, he's not, and begging him to come down only encourages him to climb further. Typical redhead"

"Reminds me of you. Not the hair but the strong headedness."

"Really? I don't remember myself climbing any jungle gyms."

"Oh, I don't know, you probably did that too, but I mean that you were the most persistent little girl I've ever seen."

"Like what?"

"Like when you got it in your head you need to get rid of Dubi, so I'll get back together with your dad."

"Oh wow, yeah, I was mean to him." Many recollections of little me yelling at Dubi that he's not my father surface as well as attempts to incite my innocent little sister against him. repeatedly refusing his help, and his gifts, all the while basking in my martyrdom and self-righteousness.

"It's understandable, You were very devoted to your dad. He loved you very much, and you felt a duty to advocate for him. You knew about his condition, you visited him in the hospital, we always told you the truth."

"Almost. Remember, you used to tell me it was a mutual decision to divorce? Even Dad backed that lie."

"I guess we didn't tell you the whole truth about that." My mom holds honesty in high regard and has a hard time admitting deceit. "I didn't want him to be seen as pitiful."

"So why did you leave him?"

She takes a deep breath, and I'm wondering if I have tissues in my handbag.

"Look, you have to understand what it was like living with him back then. He loved you and wanted to spend time with you, and I was always worried. He was overconfident and careless. I didn't trust him to take you to the pool or on a drive.

I never thought he would hurt you on purpose, he had good intentions. I was worried about his irresponsibility. On the other hand, I couldn't really talk to him. I was always maneuvering between not hurting him and not allowing him to put you at risk. It was a constant struggle."

I'm speechless and a bit ashamed. I honestly never thought about it that way. I always assumed she divorced him because she wanted a stable, healthy marriage for herself. Being the mother of a 4-year-old, it suddenly seems so clear.

"I also didn't want you to see me telling him what he could or couldn't do. I didn't want you to witness arguments. I wanted you to grow up in a calm home, to have a quiet, normal life. I didn't want you to grow up in a stressful environment. I was so wrapped up in it I didn't even consider what it meant for me as his partner."

"So how did he really take it?"

"Not well. He asked me to change my mind, He asked me to come back, promised he'd try to be quiet and give me space. He tried to come see me at my apartment, but I would ask him to leave after a cup of tea. I couldn't talk to him honestly. I couldn't tell him I don't trust him with you. I was always making excuses because I didn't want to hurt him. He really didn't deserve what happened to him. Such a good, smart, talented guy, a loving husband, and father, I felt bad for him. I don't like to use the word pity, but I felt that a horrible thing, a horrible injustice happened to him, and it wasn't his fault."

The sun went down, and a chilly breeze sprouted goosebumps on my naked arms.

I swatted a mosquito on my leg and called to my son, telling him it's time to go home. After a brief negotiation, I agreed to stay 5 more minutes.

We gathered our things, and as I watched Ben go for a last round on the swing, I asked her, "How did you decide to be open with us about everything?"

"I don't remember the decision. It's just the way I am. I believe it's best to tell children the truth in an age-appropriate way. I thought it was important you grow up understanding that mental illness is not something to ridicule. It's a disability, like other disabilities. It was important to me that you'd understand your dad is still smart and still has interests, but his personality had changed. It was also a way for me to pass on to you my belief that people with disabilities deserve respect. I was very young at the time, but I think I did well."

It's my turn to look for a tissue, and I quickly dab my eyes before hugging my son off the swing.

Eyesight

2005

It was an unusually cool August morning in the New Jersey suburbs. I made two cups of Americano and slowly sipping went to open some windows.

"Dad, come look!" I called, pointing through the glass facing the back yard.

My dad put down his coffee mug, got up from the kitchen table and came to stand by my side.

"Isn't it crazy? Look how many!" I exclaimed. Dad said nothing.

"Dad?"

He was peering through the window next to me but showed no sign of recognition.

In the back yard, a mere 100 feet from us, a flock of about 15 turkeys was parading across the lawn. Two large ones which I guessed were the parents, ugly black feathered beasts with a bruise-blue head and drooping red necks were leading the pack, followed by five or six smaller ones, last season's chicks I assumed, and a bunch of small grays, which I thought were somewhat cute.

"Tsani, you know I don't see that well anymore," Dad said apologetically.

I didn't know.

Usually, I saw my dad about once a year, when I visited Israel with my family.

That summer, I convinced him to come visit us. When I

offered to buy him the plane ticket his main concern was the 12-hour flight without smoking, but he agreed to come, armed with a supply of lemon-flavored hard candy.

For many years now Dad has been mostly stable, with an occasional short hospitalization once or twice a decade. He was living on the kibbutz, working at the car repair shop or as a minibus driver, mostly transporting elderly kibbutz members around the kibbutz or for nearby errands.

It was a pleasant visit so far. Dad helped my husband assemble a wooden swing set we bought, and my son enjoyed spending time with his grandfather, playing Lego, swinging or going to the park. In all the time I spent with my dad in recent years, I never had reason to suspect that his eyesight had significantly deteriorated.

I made myself a second coffee and sat beside him.

"I didn't know you have vision loss," I said, raising the pitch of my voice at the end of the sentence to indicate it's also an inquiry. When he didn't reply I proceeded, "Have you consulted a doctor?"

It was a rhetorical question. I knew he hadn't. My dad had a long-standing distrust- or maybe fear is a better word- of doctors and avoided them at all cost.

"Nah," he dismissed with an upward motion of the palm and explained that for sure it is just cataracts, like his mother had, and eventually he will need to have an outpatient procedure to resolve the issue. I wasn't convinced. My medical training taught me that most medical conditions are not that simple, and in my years of practicing as a veterinarian, I often saw the harmful effects of presumed diagnosis without proper testing.

I made him promise to see an ophthalmologist as soon as he gets back home.

The visit was enjoyable. We drove with another family to upstate New York and spent a couple of days in the Lake Placid area. I was constantly on the lookout for further signs of Dad's deteriorating eyesight but saw none. It didn't ease my concerns. My father was smart and good at pretending, and I was reluctant to trick-question him, lest he'll notice my ruse and get offended.

* * *

As expected, Dad did not rush to see a doctor for his eyesight when he got home. Every time I brought up the subject, he promised he would call for an appointment the next day but he never did. As he saw it, the deadline for surgery was a few years away, by his 65th birthday, when he'll be required by law to get his vision tested in order to renew his driver's license. When he eventually did go to see a doctor, he was indeed diagnosed with cataracts, but also with severe glaucoma. He began treatment for the glaucoma right away but the damage to his retina was irreversible. He had cataract surgery in one eye in 2009, but it did not improve his eyesight by much. He was pronounced legally blind and lost his driver's license.

My sister and I considered it the beginning of his end. For him, the loss of the ability to drive was like losing a limb. Or two. He stopped going to work, and barely left his apartment. He spent his days sitting in front of the TV, watching movies and listening to music.

His loss of sight is often featured in my "what-if" thoughts. There must have been a way I could have taken him to see a doctor earlier.

In the tug-of-war between letting him live his own life and pressuring him to make better decisions, we often let our end of the rope drop. Was it out of love? Wish to avoid conflict? Laziness? Probably a mix of all of those and more. A dash of each, blended in with his stubbornness, seasoned the tepid soup that was the last few years of his life.

Collapse

2006

About half an hour after we crossed the border to Maine, my phone beeped with an incoming message.

It was the first week of September, but some of the greenery along the highway was already dappled with the rust spots of the changing seasons.

"Sounds like we have reception again," Oded said at the wheel.

I flipped open the Motorola and navigated to the messages menu.

"Nits, are you still in Canada? Yair called, there's… with Dad." Dalia's voice was breaking up due to the poor connection. "The neighbors heard screaming and … smelled gas. They called the police and an ambulance. Call me when you get the message."

The timestamp was from a few hours earlier. I tried calling back, but the call went directly to voicemail.

"Shit," I mumbled.

"What's wrong?" Oded asked.

I repeated Dalia's message, and before I could finish the second sentence, I found myself sobbing. Oded, well versed in the etiquette of the weeping wife, handed over the tissue box and asked if I wanted him to pull over. I said no. I didn't want Ben in the back seat to wake up.

It has been an emotional summer. In June, on the day our embryos from the fourth IVF cycle were supposed to be transplanted, my doctor called and explained that none of the eggs developed adequately, and there was nothing to use. He said we should come in to discuss our options moving forward.

A couple of days later, at his office, Dr. Navot, friendly as usual, said that my body, in that last cycle, produced fewer eggs than before, and none of them survived the fertilization in the lab. Although I may still have a better cycle in the future, the chances are low since the overall direction of my ovaries' ability to produce eggs is down. If we wish to continue, we should consider an egg donation.

My first reaction was no way. We already went far beyond what I initially thought we would. When I first scheduled a doctor's appointment for failing to conceive, I expected to get some hormone supplements, nothing more elaborate. After all, 4 years before that, I got pregnant with Ben on the first try. I never expected to go as far as IVF. But as things often go, one thing led to another. Pills were replaced by injections, timed intercourse by artificial insemination. After an ectopic pregnancy, my doctor said that we can't continue with those, and it's either IVF or giving up. Oded was okay with stopping. He was satisfied with having just one child, but I thought it was unfair to Ben. We each have three siblings and excellent relationships with them, and being an only child seemed incredibly lonely to me. I looked into adoption, but due to our immigration status as Green Card holders, adoption from a foreign country was not an option. The doctor explained the donation process and said the donor could be a relative or an anonymous woman who would undergo extensive medical and psychological screening. We were to think about it and call him if we wished to proceed.

That evening we talked it over. I thought it was risky, having a child without knowing anything about their genetics. I didn't so much care if they looked like us, but what if they carried other genetic conditions? Oded listened patiently, but I detected an amused expression in his eyes.

"What?" I asked, baffled.

And then I realized how stupid I sounded. I was a likely carrier of a severe mental disorder. How much worse could it get?

I don't know when Dalia and I first learned of the hereditary nature of Dad's illness. Probably in our teens. And we gradually became aware of other family members on that side of the family who showed degrees of mood disorders. Naturally, we were concerned we may have inherited that trait. Later, as mothers, we worried the genes may have skipped a generation and would show up in our children. I remember one particular phone call. Dalia, not usually superstitious, brought up the fact that her oldest son was born on Dad's birthday. I thought that my son's red hair may indicate a genetic connection.

It was easy to forget about Dad's illness when he was well, but these reprieves often ended with a calamity. All things considered, it was probably at least as safe to receive an egg donation from a well-screened donor as to pass on my own genes.

The phone rang, and I answered on the first ring.

"He's okay. They got him out. He's fine." Dalia said and apologized for not answering earlier. Her baby fell asleep, so she took a short nap with her.

"You were probably worried sick. Me too."

She filled me in on the details. Yair phoned her in the early afternoon. He said someone called him just now saying they heard banging and shouting coming from Dad's apartment, and they thought they smelled gas. He was on his way there with the kibbutz nurse. Since Dalia couldn't leave the house with a newborn, she asked her husband, Avner, who was incidentally in the area for work, to go to Ein Arava and see what was happening. She just spoke to him. When he arrived at my dad's apartment, the kibbutz nurse, together with police and firefighters from the nearest town, were waiting outside and just about to go in. He went in with them. They found Dad naked, very confused.

The apartment was in horrible disarray and smelled of cooking gas. The policemen moved in to restrain and cuff Dad, although he wasn't resisting. Avner got him a blanket, covered him, and asked the police to remove the cuffs. At first, they were reluctant, but he told them he took full responsibility and was a doctor (He is one. In entomology, specializing in fruit flies).

They took him out while the firefighters checked for the gas leak. They were now on their way to the Beit Shean police.

"Why police?" I asked.

"I don't know. He couldn't talk long. He just said Dad is very confused, but he is walking on his own, and from what he could tell, he only had superficial cuts and bruises."

"Do you think he tried to kill himself?" I was finally able to say out loud what was obviously on everyone's mind. Although Dad was often depressed, I wasn't aware of him ever attempting suicide.

The baby cried in the background, and I realized I had forgotten to inquire about her. But Dalia was already saying she would call me with further updates and hung up.

We drove in silence. On the radio, someone was talking about Hurricane Katrina. It was a few days after the first anniversary of that tragedy, and I remembered how it had hit New Orleans while we were on a trip in upstate New York with my dad. He seemed so well during that visit. In a good mood, he played with Ben, just your typical grandfather. For years now, he's been doing fine. As a minibus driver, he had his "regulars" with whom he connected. They appreciated his friendliness and eagerness to help. He assisted his mom as needed and visited my sister and her family once a month.

Then earlier that summer, the State of Israel and the Hezbollah organization entered into a military conflict, later dubbed "The Second Lebanon War." Israel attacked targets in Lebanon while Hezbollah fired rockets on Israel. Some of those rockets made it as far as the Jezreel valley, and sirens alerted kibbutz members to take shelter. Dad sounded stressed on the phone and at some point, stopped answering altogether, so we weren't sure if he was home. On the day we left on our road trip, he finally answered, and we talked very briefly. After that, during most of our time in Canada, we had no cell phone reception.

I didn't hear back from Dalia that evening. In the morning, I spoke to her and got the rest of the story.

We were lucky my brother-in-law was there. When they entered the apartment, the policemen rushed to cuff dad and were ready to drag him out to the street naked. They then left it to Avner to support Dad down the stairs, keeping their distance. During the ride and later, when they waited at the police station for an ambulance, they had them sit on a bench outside, and no one offered any help or asked if they needed anything. More than once, an officer passing by made a derisive remark or motion about Dad's appearance or odor. Thankfully, Dad was probably too confused to register those comments.

Dalia sounded angry, and I joined in, exchanging words such as idiots and ignoramuses. There's a certain satisfaction in anger, and it's so much easier than imagining Dad in such a situation, or worse, admitting we were thankful we didn't have to see him in that state ourselves.

Eventually, an ambulance came and took them to the Hillel Yaffe medical center.

He had an abnormal EKG on admission, so they were running some tests, but so far, everything looked fine. He was hospitalized in the internal medicine unit and received a psych consultation. Once he was cleared medically, they planned to transfer him to their psychiatric unit. Ruth was involved and getting the medical updates.

"What do you think happened?" I asked. "Do you think he was trying to hurt himself?"

"No. I talked to Yair. From the way things were in the apartment, they don't think he opened the gas on purpose. He pulled out a pipe from the wall, and it ripped."

Dad stayed in the hospital's psychiatric ward for a couple of weeks and then went back to the kibbutz to his apartment.

* * *

As for me, in October, I called the fertility doctor and told him we would like to go ahead with the egg donation. A few weeks later, he sent me a fax with general information about a potential donor. She was of similar height and skin color as me and had no familial history of genetic disorders. By mid-winter, I was pregnant with twins, a boy and a girl.

Proper Burial

1971

The small black ball whistles by and almost hits me. It lands just next to my sandcastle and causes a small avalanche. A teen holding a paddle follows it, bends down to take it out of my offering hand, and runs back to the spot where he was playing without an apology.

"You got to watch out!" Dad yells after him, but his words dissipate in the breeze.

It's early summer. Dad and I are spending Saturday morning at the seaside. Usually, when Dad visits, we stay on the kibbutz, either in Mom's room or at my Grandparents', but today Dad offered to take me to Nahariya to see some old friends and go to the beach, and Mom agreed.

Dad helps me rebuild my sandcastle. We each grab a fistful of very wet sand from the hole we dug earlier and allow it to slowly drip over the sides, creating irregularly rounded clumps and thin spikes.

Dad lights a cigarette and I make a face. I heard adults say smoking is unhealthy, and anyway, I don't like the smell. The wind carries the smoke in my direction, and I take a handful of sand and aim it at the burning end. "Tsani!" Dad says, surprised. Turns out I'm a better aim than I thought, and the barely smoked cigarette is now doused with sand.

"Sorry," I mumble. I really didn't mean to do that.

"It's alright," Dad says, "but it was an important cigarette, the last in the pack, and now it's dead. We need to give it a proper burial."

We walk to the edge of the beach looking for an appropriate spot and settle on a patch of sand under some low thorny shrubs. Dad is holding the deceased, and I'm looking for suitable headstone material. Among the debris scattered around, I find an almost intact square tile and a piece of charcoal left over from someone's campfire.

We dig a hole, and Dad places the cigarette in it, then gingerly covers it.

"What should it say?" he asks.

"Rest in peace, cigarette," I say, and Dad uses the coal to write it on the slab. He gives it to me, and I place it ceremoniously over the sand. I almost manage to keep a straight face.

A man with a large white box hanging from his neck is trudging through the sand, calling, "Ice Cream, Ice-pops, Lemon, Watermelon, Vanilla, Chocolate." Dad nods his chin in his direction, then takes my hand, and we hurry to catch up to him.

Lithium

2010

The answering machine picked up on the 6th ring. "This. Is. the. Home. Of. Saul. Lavie. Please. Leave. a. message." my dad's voice said, articulating each word separately, with the deliberate stiffness reserved for recorded announcements.

It's been more than a week since Dad last picked up the phone, and yet I wasn't overly concerned. He's been mostly depressed for a while now, since his unsuccessful cataract surgery and the loss of his driving license, but he managed, spending his days in his apartment, in bed, or in front of the TV. Sometimes unwilling or unable to answer calls.

In a couple of days, I will be able to visit him. It was the beginning of summer vacation, and we were going with our 10 years old son and toddler twins to Israel for 3 weeks.

The day before the flight, my sister called. Yair went to check on Dad and found him in bad shape.

"Bad shape how?" I asked; images of a stroke, heart attack, and other afflictions of aging, heavy smoking, and sedentary lifestyle flooded my imagination.

She wasn't clear on the details, but they were taking him to Shaar Menashe, a psychiatric hospital.

"So they think it's just a bad bout of depression?" I asked, relieved.

"I'm not sure," she said. "I guess."

The next day we arrived in Israel. On the way from the airport, the twins fell asleep in their car seats, and I took the opportunity to call Dalia.

She told me that when Dad was admitted to the hospital, he was dehydrated and had some abnormal blood test results, so he was transferred to a nearby medical center. He was hospitalized in the internal medicine unit. Between work and caring for her 4 children, she wasn't sure when she'd be able to visit. I told her not to worry about it; I would go first thing in the morning.

My phone alarm woke me up at 8 am AKA 1 o'clock in the morning, New Jersey time. By my calculations, the rest of my jet-lagged family would probably sleep until noon or later, so they wouldn't miss me.

I took a couple of minutes to figure out the coffee machine while my brain begged to go back to bed, but once the caffeine hit my bloodstream, the prospect of the day ahead seemed significantly brighter.

After 12 years living in a US suburb, I was no longer used to the chaos that pervades most Israeli public spaces. The entrance was swarming with patients and families, and there was no information desk in sight. I skimmed the numerous incongruous signs in Hebrew, English, and Arabic until I located the sign saying, "Internal Medicine - 2nd Floor."

The elevator door opened into a yellowish hallway, reeking of disinfectants and a stale mix of body odors and food. The nurses' station was abandoned. I waited, not sure what else to do. Peering into rooms in search of my dad seemed like an invasion of privacy.

Finally, a nurse materialized, walking briskly past me, and it took a few "excuse me-s" to get her attention.

At first, I thought that in her rush, she gave me the wrong room number. Or maybe I misheard her. Neither of the men in the beds looked like Dad. Then I recognized him, and I felt like I was in one of those science fiction movies when people illogically, suddenly age. He looked like he was 90, frail, his skin grayish and brittle. I walked up to him. His eyes were closed. He was connected to an IV line, and an EKG monitor beeped softly next to him.

"Dad?" I said quietly, not sure if he was sleeping or just ignoring his surroundings. He opened his eyes and looked in my direction. I couldn't tell if he recognized me. He tried to talk, but I couldn't understand what he was saying. It was more like sounds sprinkled with occasional words than sentences.

I pulled a chair from the corner of the room and sat next to him, my hand on his arm. Unsure of his cognitive state, I spoke to him slowly, hoping he could understand.

"Dad, it's me, Nitsan. You are in the hospital, in Hillel-Yaffe. You were dehydrated, so you're getting fluids. We arrived yesterday. Remember I told you we are exchanging houses with that family in Binyamina?" He may have nodded, then closed his eyes again.

There was a clipboard fixed to the end of the bed. I tried to make sense of the treatment instructions, but the unfamiliar abbreviations threw me off. I sat there for a little longer, playing the role of the dutiful daughter when all I really wanted to do was to find out more medical details. I get like this during emergencies; practical, detached, focused on problem-solving. As a vet, I thrive on it; the adrenalin high from an unfolding crisis, the ability to function efficiently under stressful conditions. At home, I pride myself on being cool-headed, able to assess injury or illness even when it involves my own children. A therapist once suggested that it's a defense mechanism I'd developed early on. Maybe she was right. How else would a little girl deal with seeing her dad at a mental hospital? It's not that I don't feel anything; I just store those feelings away for later, when the crisis is averted and safety restored. Then they sneak back, crawling out of a dark hole in the middle of the night, wearing the form of "what ifs," red and yellow venomous snakes of worse-case scenarios, and guilt over actions not taken.

I went to look for someone who could give me some medical information.

This time there was a nurse at the desk, but she couldn't tell me much. Only that Dad was being treated for dehydration, and lab work was pending. She said that later or the next day they will probably know more.

As soon as I got in the car, I called my sister. "He looks awful," I said. "He's... I don't know, just awful... He looks old, thin, weak. He couldn't even talk." I blinked hard, pushing back on the tears pooling in the corners of my eyes.

"Shit," she said, "Do they know what's wrong with him?"

"The nurse said he's dehydrated. They are waiting on more tests, I guess. Honestly, if it was just dehydration, I'd expect him to be better by now. He's been on fluids for what? At least 12 hours?"

"Maybe I can leave work early and see if someone can pick up Inbar and Oren..." she was thinking-out-loud. She, too, prefers to deal with practicalities than dwell on worries.

"Don't jump through hoops for it; I'm not even sure he knew I was there. It's a long drive from your place. I'll go again tomorrow."

We talked a little more about other things. Mainly our plans for getting together on the weekend and who would call Grandma with an update on Dad. We hung up. But a dark cloud of unspoken doubts lingered.

The next day Oded's niece came to babysit the twins, and he went with me to the hospital. When we entered the room, Dad was propped up in bed and looked more alert than yesterday. I approached him, and he smiled and said, "Tsani!"

Oded, behind me, said, "Hi Saul, how are you?"

Dad looked at him and slurred, "Are you her brother?"

I managed to keep a straight, smiling face while my brain exploded with 'Damn it. Shit. Damn it'."

We sat with Dad for a little while. He talked a bit. It wasn't all clear and didn't all make sense, but I saw a vast improvement from the day before and assumed it was just a matter of time.

When Dad asked for water by pointing to an orange plastic jug by his bed, I poured it and handed him a cup. He attempted to hold it, but instead of putting his palms to the cup, he tried to grab it with his knuckles. To me, that looked like a sign of proprioception impairment, an indicator of neurological deficit. In dogs, we evaluate this by holding the top of the feet next to the exam table's edge. A healthy dog will instinctively flip the foot over, placing it with the footpads down in a normal walking position. Neurological deficits are caused by Central Nerve System pathology. Trauma, stroke, infections, or tumors are the most common conditions. Severe dehydration can cause dizziness, loss of balance, speech difficulties, and maybe even confusion, but I didn't think it could cause proprioception injury.

I held the cup to Dad's lips and helped him drink, and then asked Oded to stay while I went to look for a doctor.

After some haggling with the nurse, she agreed to show me to the doctor's office.

The doctor, a young resident, was abrupt.

"What's the patient's name?" she asked without any pleasantries. Again, I was reminded of the Israeli directness (that's me being generous. Rudeness and lack of basic manners would be a better description).

"He had an elevated level of Lithium when he was first admitted. He was also dehydrated. Probably wasn't drinking enough. We stopped his Lithium and are giving him fluids." She clicked on another document, "His levels are normal today. We are going to send him back to Shaar Menashe tonight," she concluded and went back to whatever she was doing before, essentially dismissing me.

"Excuse me, Doctor," I refused to leave. "He is really not Okay, he is completely neurological..." in my incredulity, I forgot how to talk "Medical" and probably sounded a bit daft. "I just gave him a glass of water, and he held it with the back of his hands," I demonstrated, "There has to be some neurological deficit, lack of proprioception, I'm a medical professional (avoid saying Veterinarian or they'll say something derisive about animals)."

"Look," said the doctor, "he was dehydrated when he came here. There seems to be some neglect. He needs better care, but we are a medical facility; it's not our job."

"You don't understand," I tried again. "He is 66, he is strong and independent, this is not normal," but I could already tell she wasn't listening. All she saw in Dad was an elderly mental patient, and now she was blaming me, us, for failing to care for him.

Elyn Saks, an esteemed professor of law and psychiatry who lives with schizophrenia, talks about an ER visit in her book The Center Cannot Hold. Elyn, then a graduate student, developed severe headaches, nausea, and confusion. Her friends came to check on her and got concerned.

"Quickly, they bundled me into their car and took me to the emergency room where a completely predictable disaster happened: The ER discovered that I had a psychiatric history. And that was the end of any further diagnostic work.

Stigma against mental illness is a scourge with many faces, and the medical community wears a number of those faces." Saks writes. "Poor Maria was literally jumping up and down, trying to tell anyone who'd listen that she had seen me psychotic before and that this was different. But her testimony didn't help because I was a mental patient. The ER sent me away."

Later, with the intervention of her internist, she was admitted for testing and diagnosed with a life-threatening brain aneurism.

I read the book years after my father passed away and immediately identified with Maria, "jumping up and down" to no avail.

I found my way back to my dad's room, all wired up and ready to fight, only there was no one to wrestle with other than stigma and apathy toward the mentally afflicted, which is deep-rooted in our society.

"You wouldn't believe it, those morons," I said to Oded and recounted the conversation.

"Why won't you call Ruth or Dubi," Oded suggested. "They'll probably listen to them, you know, doctor to doctor?"

I kissed Dad goodbye and promised to come to see him the next day.

On the way back, I tried to call Ruth, but there was no answer. I left her a message, saying that Dad is not well and that I don't think he is getting proper care and maybe she can intervene. Next, I called Dubi. He answered right away. I described Dad's situation in detail.

"So they think it's Lithium toxicity caused by dehydration?" He asked.

"Yes, but today his Lithium level is within the therapeutic range, and he still has neurological symptoms."

Dubi said he doesn't remember much about Lithium toxicity, but he will look it up when he gets home. We planned to see them later anyway.

When we got to my parents' house with the kids in the afternoon, a heavy medical textbook was already open on the dining room table.

After giving each kid a kiss and a hug, Dubi said he thinks he found something.

"Read here." He pointed to a paragraph and without waiting for me to review it proceeded to summarize, "It says that in cases of chronic toxicity, and it makes sense that his case is chronic, he probably continued to take his regular dose, but because of dehydration his body wasn't clearing it, there is intracellular Lithium accumulation, and even after blood levels seem normal there is still excess Lithium in the body."

Lithium, a trace element, has been used in medicine since the 19th century. In 1949, an Australian psychiatrist, John Cade, published a paper describing the successful use of Lithium in the treatment of mania. Since the early seventies, Lithium salts have been the mainstay of mood-stabilizing treatment of bipolar disorder. My dad has been taking Lithium regularly since early in his disease, and I remember him telling me it saved his life, and he could not function without it. Lithium has a narrow therapeutic range, meaning that the effective but not toxic blood level is rather specific and needs to be closely monitored. Mild toxicity can cause stomach upset and nausea; severe toxicity will manifest as a range of neurological and systemic abnormalities and might even lead to death. The key treatment in cases of toxicity is intravenous fluids that help clear the body of excess Lithium before cautiously resuming the medication.

I agreed with Dubi that the chronic accumulation of Lithium in the cells is a probable explanation for Dad's normal blood levels despite his clinical signs. Dubi said that the attending doctors must have left for the day, but he would try to call in the morning.

That evening, lying in bed unable to fall asleep, I scanned in my head the list of Lithium side effects: diarrhea, vomiting, fatigue, drowsiness, tremors, seizures. I could envision a possible scenario of Dad developing diarrhea maybe, becoming dehydrated but continuing to take his dependable medicine, getting weaker and sicker and unable to drink, lying in bed, physically and mentally unable to call for help. How long has he been ill now, while we assumed it was just his usual depression and left him alone?

Did we fail him? Was it our fault that he got to this point? Who should have noticed? How can I expect other family members to be responsible when I'm sitting comfortably in New Jersey?

Dubi phoned me the next day to say that apparently Dad was sent back to the psychiatric hospital first thing in the morning. Annoyed and concerned, I called them. I was put on hold for a while as a nurse tried to locate him or his psychiatrist. She finally got back on the line and told me that the doctor sent him back to the medical center because he was obviously not well.

I was relieved and thankful that the psychiatrist saw his condition as I did and insisted on continued medical care.

Over the next couple of days Dad got better. He was able to get up, first with help and then by himself. His speech became clearer, and he regained his memory, although the events of the last week remained blurry. Probably for the best. When he eventually did go back to the psych ward, the psychiatrist said that he should never take Lithium again. The medication he depended on for decades was now poisonous.

Home

November 2011

My uncle parked the car with two wheels on the sidewalk, as close to my dad's apartment entrance as possible without risking a flat tire.

I got out of the back seat into the blinding noon sun and went around to open the passenger door where my father sat, motionless. He turned his head slowly but showed no intention to get out.

"One minute, Tsani," he said, slouched in the seat as if the only thing holding him upright was the seatbelt he didn't bother to unfasten.

The air, like my father, was still. The dusty ground and the silence made it feel like we'd landed on the moon. Had we?

The sound of the trunk popping startled me. My uncle took out the tattered luggage and carried it up the ten stairs to the door, while I waited for my dad to indicate he was ready to follow.

I didn't want to rush him.

It was his first time out of the psychiatric hospital in over a year.

The summer before last, after recovering from the Lithium toxicity, Dad went back and they tried to treat him with other medications.

Israel has a state funded health care system. It has its strengths, like the fact that there is no insurance company pressure to keep hospital stays short. However, care options are limited, even if one has financial means. A psychiatric patient is assigned to a specific hospital based on their residency address, and to a ward based on the severity of their illness and their stage in life.

My father was assigned to the geriatric ward at the "Sha'ar Menashe" regional psychiatric hospital. During his first week there, his doctor put him on an antidepressant, but it made him agitated, and after he pushed another patient, the medication was stopped, and he remained severely depressed. My sister and I tried to talk to his doctor multiple times but got no concrete answers. It seemed like the staff was satisfied keeping my father, and the rest of the patients, quiet and complacent. We were not.

We decided to take him home. We didn't have any secret weapon to treat his depression, but we thought he'd be better off in the comfort of his own apartment, living by his own rules, surrounded by his own things and not subject to the strict schedule and forced company of the ward. His siblings objected; they thought he should stay in the hospital. I wasn't sure if for his own good or for theirs.

I flew from New Jersey to Israel to take my dad home and help him acclimate. I thought he'd be glad, but he was terrified, and I couldn't understand why.

Finally, he made a move to turn in the seat, but the seatbelt held him back. He sat himself up and fumbled for the latch. Exposed and vulnerable, his right foot reached the sidewalk, looking for solid ground. With my uncle's help, we got him out of the car. Sixty-seven years old, he looked and moved like a man in his 80s.

He slowly pulled himself up the stairs, hanging tight to the railing. I climbed behind him, ready to catch him if he tottered. He reached the door and, leaning his weight on it, pushed it open.

A musty smell of mildew and old cigarettes greeted him with "welcome home," but he didn't reply. He just stood there, and I thought to myself that maybe the whole idea was a colossal mistake. What did I get myself into? What did we do to him?

Without a word, he walked into the living room and began inspecting his abandoned kingdom. In the decades he'd lived there alone, he'd built himself an improvised elaborate entertainment center. Three TV stands stood in a row, supporting two TV screens and a dozen other electronics. I saw two DVD players, a DVR, a cable box, a sound amplifier, and a CD player. An electrician's nightmare of wires ran on the floor like a snake pit in an Indiana Jones movie, connecting the machines to each other and electricity. He began inspecting the connections and turning on devices. I offered to help, but he brushed me off, so I went to check on the rest of the apartment.

It was the long-forsaken abode of an elderly man, with severely declining eyesight, who never employed a cleaning person and took care of any repairs by himself. To say that it was in dreadful disarray would be an understatement. I inspected the white paint peeling off a kitchen cabinet door, then slid it open to expose a minimal selection of cooking utensils thrown haphazardly on an uncovered shelf, hibernating in a layer of dust and paint chips. A dead beetle extended 6 skinny legs upward in surrender. In the adjacent cabinet, I found a collection of screwdrivers, hammers, wires, and other work tools I couldn't name.

Above the kitchen sink, the green wall tiles were cracked in places and sealed off by an ugly patchwork of browning plaster or glue. A sticky layer of burnt oil splatters surrounded the hot plate.

"Tsani," Dad called me, so I made a mental list of everything I'll need to take care of in the coming week and went to see how he was doing.

He was sitting in his armchair, the remote in one hand, a cigarette in the other, flipping channels.

"Do you want to watch a movie?"

For the first time that day, a sliver of hope penetrated my doubt, but it was only transient.

I slept at my grandma›s and arrived early the next morning to find my dad already staring at the TV. He said he didn›t sleep much at night, and after a small breakfast, he went back to bed. He stayed there most of the day while I embarked on the gargantuan cleaning and arranging project. Manuel, a home-aid who took care of another elderly person in the kibbutz, came to meet us in the afternoon. My sister hired him to stop by twice a day to take care of my dad›s needs once I'm gone. A heavyset guy, with an Argentinian accent and pleasant smile, he sat down, and we talked practicalities. When we were through with the details, I asked if he'd help me take Dad on a walk. But Dad refused. I tried everything; enticement, and pressure, pleading and negotiation, to no avail. In the following days, I tried again and again but was unable to persuade him.

My dad had no diagnosed neurological or muscular diseases, and yet he was as weak and unstable as an octogenarian. I was convinced it was due to years of inertia and resolved to reverse it, little by little, with physical activity. I could not fathom his resistance. He seemed terrified to go out, but why? I tried to understand, to find a logical explanation: "Are you afraid of running into someone you know and don't want to face? Are you afraid of falling on the steps?" I suggested, convinced that once I identified the root of the fear, I could weed it out. He answered no to my questions but did not offer clarification.

Years later, when my dad was no longer with us, I came across the book "Darkness Visible" by William Styron. In it, Styron describes his struggle with depression.

"I felt loss at every hand. The loss of self-esteem is a celebrated symptom, and my own sense of self had all but disappeared, along with any self-reliance. This loss can quickly degenerate into dependence, and from dependence into infantile dread. One dreads the loss of all things, all people close and dear. There

is an acute fear of abandonment. Being alone in the house, even for a moment, caused me exquisite panic and trepidation."

Reading it, I realized I never actually understood what depression is.

Growing up with a bipolar father, the manic episodes were impossible to ignore. When in "high mode,» he was active and talkative, demanding, and potentially embarrassing. Mania brings on outrageous events, sometimes funny, infuriating, or scary, but always conspicuous. Dad would call us a few times a day, weave intricate plans, divulge that he was writing a book or opening a business. He would show up unannounced, or run away with a "borrowed" car, spinning tornadoes of worry all around.

Depression, however, is quiet and invisible, like the blurry object in the background of a photograph. We knew it was there, but we didn't really know what it was, so it was easy to ignore. The depressed person prefers to avoid, to stay away. Dad would refuse visits, or cut them short, disregard the ringing phone, or the knock on the door. In turn, we would tell ourselves that we respect his wishes and walk away, allowing him to further sink into the nothingness.

It's not that I didn't want to understand depression. I thought that I did. I imagined it akin to deep sadness, or loss, so I couldn't grasp the other aspects of it, the fear and self-loathing. In recent years I came to suspect that a large part of the misconception of depression lies in the word itself.

The fact that we use the phrase so casually to describe a reaction to any small unfortunate event, "I'm so depressed, I got a B in math," Or to talk about something serious, "This show is so depressing," depreciates the meaning of it. We confuse melancholy with clinical depression, and assuming we understand, never look deeper.

The rest of the week progressed slowly. I cleaned, organized, shopped, and spent as much time with my dad as he allowed, which wasn't much. I also photographed him, his apartment, the kibbutz, and an occasional stray cat. Photography is my hobby and therapy, and it allowed me to detach myself from the situation a bit. In many of my photographs, Dad is in bed, covered in a blanket up to his chin, his back turned to me, and all you can see of him is a scalp of spiky white hair.

My Brother's Keeper

2016

Dalia and I wrapped up the interview with Deborah and, not bothering to fully pack my video equipment, carried it over to Yair's house, less than 100 yards away.

Leah, Yair's wife, opened the door wearing a floral-print shirt, and light blue glasses, her dark hair in a ponytail. After offering us a cold drink, she suggested we set up in the living room.

Yair joined us a couple of minutes later. He is a squat man, and with his unruly forelock of salt and pepper hair, greatly resembles Ezra, his father. He wore a short-sleeved button-down, dark blue shirt, and a two-day stubble.

"What do you want to ask me about?" he inquired while I was still setting up.

"I don't know, not anything specific, more like what you remember from Dad, from when you were young, and maybe about some specific events that we are trying to understand."

"Well, you know, as children, we didn't really..." he began.

I stopped him and asked if he could wait until I was done setting up the camera.

Leah asked if we would mind if she listened in. I suggested she join the interview, but she said no and sat on an armchair out of camera range.

"So you began telling me about your childhood," I prompted once ready.

"You know, we weren't a close family. Ezra wasn't big on the family doing things together. I don't remember any family dinners or anything like that. I remember once, I did something bad at school; I don't remember what, and the punishment was to sleep in my parents' home for a night. Ezra made a big stink of it; he was angry and said it wasn't in line with kibbutz rules. He was a fanatic like that. The only occasion I remember spending time with Saul was when we visited the cousins in Ashkelon. We went to the beach, which was a big deal for us. Then, in '58, Uri was born, and things got more difficult."

"What else do you remember from the early years?" I ask, hoping for more.

"I remember when he met Alona on a trip from Oranim or something. And Ezra didn't want to go to the wedding in the rabbinical center. At the last minute, a friend convinced him to go."

Grandpa Ezra was known to have a strong objection to the religious establishment in Israel. No one in the family was a practicing Jew; however, the only authority licensed to perform marriages in Israel was, and still is, orthodox rabbis (And probably Muslim or Christian religious officials for non-Jewish persons). Hence, the default for most couples is to marry in a Jewish ceremony. Years later, I remember him referring to my cousin's circumcision as a pagan antiquated ceremony. I tend to agree.

"Then he was in the Six Day War and shortly after in Karameh, and that's when he had the first collapse. I don't know exactly what happened. Shmulik Pasternik or Avi Rimon would probably know more. They were there; you should talk to them." Yair jumped ahead in time.

"Was there any sign of anything wrong with him before that?" I asked.

Yair shook his head. "No, I don't think so. But I remember when it began. He would yell in the middle of the kibbutz or in the Dining Room—really loud. He was never physically violent, but he was loud and behaved... you could see. He changed. People were afraid of him."

All of a sudden, I realized that Yair was barely 20 years old at the time. I can only imagine what it was like to watch his intelligent, dependable older brother behave like a crazy person in front of the entire kibbutz—the horror and the embarrassment of it. Did he ever move past it?

"Karameh was what? January of '68? So, it began in the summer after. Dalia was just born. Grandpa Ezra would sometimes take her to the Children's House in the evening to help your mom. I had an American girlfriend then, and I remember taking care of you. You were what? 2 or 3?" Yair asked, addressing me.

"Sometimes, we needed to force-hospitalize him. They calmed him down there, and after a while, he was discharged. But the first years were tough. Really tough. I could understand why Alona had difficulty living with him, but Ezra couldn't. He never forgave her. That's why when she married Dubi, we asked them not to stay in Ein Arava.

Then there was that time when Grandma Anna bought him a TV set, and he traded it for a Vespa, and Ezra got mad and tried to sabotage it. Saul rode that Vespa everywhere. At his funeral one of his classmates said he saw Saul with the Vespa in Sinai during the Yom Kippur war. He drove all over Sinai in the middle of everything. When you're manic, you think you are invincible; you do crazy things. But then comes the depression," Yair paused without elaborating. "What else do you want to know? Ask something."

"Do you remember anything about a trial?" I asked.

"While he was in Mazra?" Leah interjected.

"Trial? For what? Driving? I remember visiting him in Mazra, but no trial." Yair said.

"He once told me that he was sentenced to stay in Mazra for a period of time for impersonating a soldier and taking a weapon. Deborah remembers going to court also, but no details." I explained.

"No, I don't remember. He wouldn't steal a weapon; that

wasn't like him. Maybe he found it? I found and took things sometimes…" Yair chuckled, shrugging.

"This whole thing with forced hospitalizations was very…" Leah began but let the sentence trail off, finishing instead with a slight shoulder forward movement and tightening of the lips, a gesture of sad helplessness.

I asked her if she would move into the frame next to Yair and this time she obliged and moved over to the couch. Conscience of the camera, she smoothed out her black bangs and adjusted her glasses.

"What do you remember?" I prompted her.

"For me, the most significant memory isn't of any of the dramatic events. It was the time he called me in the middle of the night and said, 'I'm so scared, please help me,' and I was helpless; I didn't know what to do."

A heavy silence fell on the room. I don't know what the others were thinking, but I thought of all the times Dad needed my help, and I didn't know what to do.

"But he also had long stretches of good years through the '80s and '90s." Yair broke the spell. "He lived on the kibbutz and worked regularly. He had great technical skills. Whenever I needed something fixed, he did it. Me? I can't even hammer a nail properly, so I would call him to help."

"Did you have a close relationship with Dad as adults?" I asked Yair.

"Well, he picked me up from the airport when I flew to Turkey, and I drove him when he flew to visit you in 2005, so yes, I think we were okay. It was not a deep friendship, but okay."

"And on the kibbutz, did he have friends?"

"Look," Yair said in a somewhat defiant tone, "People are squeamish about people like him. And he wasn't… he was a loner; he wasn't looking for friendships. There are other people like that on the kibbutz who are only close to their families.

There are also people who are Bipolar and have better control," Yair continued. "When they feel it coming, they disappear for a while. Saul didn't, and he scared people. When you're depressed, no one knows anything, but when you're manic and you yell in the dining room, you destroy your reputation. Very few people kept in touch. In recent years I think it was just Abigail and Yossi. But during the good years, he was in contact with people all day. Remember the years he worked as a kibbutz driver? He would pick up the dentist a couple of times a week, and he had his regular passengers, some students that he drove to school; everyone always said how nice and helpful he was, that he was always on time, and if you had to go somewhere that wasn't on his regular route he would still drive you."

A minute ago, Yair said that Dad wasn't interested in friendships with people on the kibbutz. I think he was wrong. Dad very much sought connections with people, which is why he tried to be extra nice and helpful as a driver. Maybe it was easier for him to have those transient connections in the pre-determined space and time of the minibus ride than to risk true friendships, those that might disappoint him or make him feel bad about himself when he disappointed them.

"Overall, he was lucky to have the kibbutz," Yair concluded. "He always had a place to return to, an apartment. It wasn't in great shape, but it was a place."

"What did you do with everything that was there? You said you had to clear it out." Dalia asked.

"Yes, we put everything in boxes. You can go over it tomorrow. There are some framed photos, some junk, and some tools."

"He was great with fixing things," Leah commented.

"Any letters?" I asked. One can always hope.

"Maybe. I don't know. Maybe some medical documents," Yair replied.

"He had a great memory," Leah added. This has become less

of an interview and more of a conversation, Aunt and Uncle reminiscing about the deceased with the bereaved daughters. But I gave up on learning anything new, so I went along with it.

"They say that Bipolar mostly affects people with very high IQ. He had a high IQ, so maybe that's why it happened to him." Yair said. "But I don't know if it would have still happened if he didn't see what he saw in the war. Maybe if what happened in the war hadn't happened, it wouldn't have started. There was another guy here...he also had it. After a few years, he gave up and killed himself, hung himself in his apartment."

"Dad was never suicidal," I said.

"He never spoke about it, but he was often despondent," Yair said.

"Despair, yes, but I never heard him talk about suicide or say that he wanted to die," I insisted.

"Whenever I took him to the psychiatrists, they always asked if he thinks about suicide," Dalia said. She was the one who took him to doctors in later years when he couldn't drive himself anymore. "And his usual answer was that, of course, he thinks about it, but he doesn't have the courage. He often said things like 'What a pitiful life' or 'I'm pitiful.'"

"Do you think he would have coped better if Mom had stayed with him or Rachel?" I asked.

"Maybe. It helps when you are not alone," Yair answered, "especially when you're depressed and anxious."

"With all the difficulties, I see a positive story here," Leah said.

"In what way?" I asked. A bit surprised.

"I think it's unusual for a mentally ill person to have children that care so much. You could have easily distanced yourselves from him. He also had a mother and brother who were always there for and supported him. Some people give up. It's not a small thing. I'm not saying that anyone should expect a medal, but..."

"Some families put a person like that in an institute," Yair interrupted, cutting into her words, "and that's it. He was lucky that the kibbutz also helped by letting him return no matter what happened."

He was right. Living near New York City, I often see men who resemble my father. Sometimes to the point that I have to turn and take another look. I see them on the ramp leading to the George Washington Bridge, holding a sign. I see them on the sidewalk, sitting on cardboard, their meager belongings in a small pile that also serves as a pillow at night. I see them in the headlines "Large American cities, including Los Angeles, San Francisco, and New York, are struggling to deal with a growing homelessness crisis," and in politician speeches, urging housing reforms or referring to the homeless as a vermin problem that requires swift cleaning of the streets. The statistics on the prevalence of mental illness among the chronically homeless varies in numbers between different sources, but it consistently shows a 5-fold or more prevalence of mental illness among homeless people compared to the general population. And the causes are clear. Many people living with mental illness have a hard time keeping a job over the years, and often, their families give up on helping them or are unable or unwilling to house them.

Despite some shortcomings, the kibbutz allowed my dad uncommon privileges: a free-of-charge apartment, to which he could return even if the last time he was there he was unstable, access to various services, and a place of work that didn't require applications and background checks and allowed him to come back even if he previously left without notice.

The four of us chatted a bit longer about nothing in particular. Leah asked about my kids, I showed her pictures and asked about her grandchildren. Dalia wrote down some names of kibbutz members who might be able to tell us more about Dad, and we parted.

Surprise

2012

With the limited understanding of depression I had at the time, I hoped that the comfort of home would revitalize Dad.

But despite being home, in his own apartment, with his armchair, TV, and coffee machine, Dad's depression did not get any better. Compounded by severe visual impairment, dad was increasingly dependent on aid.

After a while it seemed like Manuel's twice a day visits were not enough and we replaced him with Joon, a full time Filipino caregiver. A small guy, quick to smile and eager to serve, he was an efficient worker and pleasant company for Dad, but also enabled him in his depression-induced inertia. He served him like a domestic in a movie set in the Old South, anticipating his every wish and hurrying to fulfill it. Dad had only to reach his hand toward the pack of smokes on the shelf beside him, for Joon to jump up and light his cigarette for him.

Yair stopped by every day on his walking workout around the kibbutz, to help with any practicalities. Grandma came once a week, bringing homemade cookies. Dad did not object to her visits but usually made it clear that he didn't have the energy to chat and would cut her stay short. Abigail, one of the few people outside the family who kept in touch with him, told me years later that he asked her not to visit.

I called almost every day, but our conversations were invariably short. Dad said he was tired and didn't feel like talking.

Occasionally he complained that he couldn't see much or that his legs hurt.

I again tried to convince him to go out a bit, to let Joon take him on a short walk, just around the block. He ended most conversations with the promise that he would go for a walk the next day, but he never did.

Meanwhile, my sister tried to find him a local psychiatrist. It wasn't easy. There aren't that many working in the area where he lives, and the ones there are very busy. We finally managed to get him an appointment and my sister took him to see her. She was pleasant and thorough and suggested adding a new medicine that might help with his depression. She gave us a follow-up appointment in a month. A couple of days after he began taking the new medication, Dad sounded unusually subdued when I called. He spoke slowly, and it was hard to understand him. Although I didn't get every word, I thought he might also be confused.

I called my sister, and she said she will try to get in touch with his psychiatrist. We suspected it was an adverse reaction to the new medicine, but as a medical practitioner myself, I didn't want to discontinue it without talking to the doctor first. Maybe it's a common side effect of the first days and will get better? Perhaps we should lower the dose but not discontinue? We weren't able to reach the psychiatrist. My sister left messages with her secretary, but no one called us back.

2 days later, I woke up in the morning to find a message on my phone. My sister said Dad was unable to get out of bed that morning, that the caretaker found him in wet sheets, unable to get up or talk. They took him to the emergency room, and he was hospitalized for testing. I called her back, and she updated me that he was about the same. The attending internist suspected that one of his pills was causing severe neurological impairment, and they stopped all his medications. I wasn't sure

that it was a great idea, but obviously, I wasn't there and had no say.

The following day, as I was driving back home after dropping my son off at school, my phone rang. It was my sister.

"Nits, are you up yet? I'm here with Dad; he's been anxious to speak with you."

Before I could reply, I heard a familiar voice on the phone, a voice I haven't heard in years, my dad in a cheerful mood.

"Tsani, hi, how's everything? I'm at the Afula hospital, but I'm feeling great. Dalia is here; I've been waiting for hours to call you; my cell phone's at home. How are you?"

Startled, I realized I just drove through a red light; luckily, the intersection was empty.

"Dad? You sound great! We were so worried about you."

My dad went on, telling me again how great he feels and making plans to go home and for my sister to bring her children to visit on the weekend.

Meanwhile, I got home, but I remained sitting in my car, hesitant to disconnect the phone from the hands-free set, afraid that if the call disconnects, the magic will disappear.

We spoke, or rather Dad talked mostly, for a few more minutes and then we agreed to talk again later.

My sister got on the line, and all I could say was, "What the hell...?"

She started laughing.

"Is he manic?"

"I'm not sure; but he is definitely in a good mood."

The next day dad was released from the hospital and went back home. Due to his ongoing health problems, he could not go out on his own, so he spent most of his time watching TV and listening to music. I called him almost every day, and we chatted about different things. He often reminded me of past events, places we'd been together, funny stories from my childhood, or situations in which he helped me as an adult. Despite his other issues, Dad's memory remained phenomenal. He could recall dates of any event, names, locations. He also remembered every film he ever watched and could name all the actors in it.

One such conversation stuck in my head. It went something like this:

"What are you watching?" I asked after he lowered down the volume on what sounded like a war movie.

"Twister," he said. "They have it on cable this month. Have you watched it? With Bill Paxton and Helen Hunt?"

"Yes, I saw it in a movie theater," I recalled.

"Bill Paxton is pretty good, although I liked him better in Apollo 13, but Helen Hunt is the real star here. Do you like her?"

"I do. Oded and I saw her in a Broadway play once with John Turturro and that guy who played Data on Star Track." I told him.

"Her best film was As Good As it Gets. Have you seen it?"

"Of course," I replied, "with Jack Nicholson. He's an amazing actor."

There was quiet on the line, and for a moment, I thought the connection was lost, but then Dad said, "I remember the first time I watched "Cuckoo's Nest." It was in 75. Not long after the first time I received shock treatment."

"You received shock treatments? I didn't know that." I said, surprised, afraid to ask for details.

He told me he'd received ECT for depression several times. The first time was without anesthesia and was a terrifying experience. He went on to tell me the treatment did help with his depression, and although it did cause temporary memory loss, he doesn't think it affected him long-term.

Every day I called with apprehension. Day after day, I listened closely for signs of change, hints of the good mood dissipating, the magic disintegrating.

At first, because of the abrupt and unusual, medically

impossible way it happened, I didn't expect it to last for more than a couple of days. How I wished for it to endure, but I was too experienced with this disease to fool myself. It wasn't a question of if. It was a question of when, of how long. I had no illusion this reprieve would go on forever, but as time went by, I allowed myself to hope it would extend for a few more weeks at least.

In a little over a month, we were scheduled to go to Israel, my family and I, to celebrate my son's Bar Mitzvah. When we planned the event, Dad was so depressed I had no expectation of him being there, but now that the possibility crept into my imagination, it was hard to shush it down. I asked him if he would come, and he said most definitely. It's been years since my dad participated in a family event. Was it actually going to happen?

We landed in Israel on Thursday, December 20th, and went to my in-laws' house first. We spent the night there, and early Friday morning, while my family still slept off the jet lag, I drove by myself to see Dad. I also brought my camera with me.

A few months earlier I began taking videography classes, a somewhat natural extension of my photography hobby. The course syllabus went beyond the use of video equipment to include the basics of filmmaking. While my first students' film was a short fictional story starring my son, I already knew that my real interest was in documentary work, and trying to compose my dad's story was a natural starting point for me. I asked Dad ahead of time if he would be willing to be interviewed on camera and he said yes. When we discussed my visit, he asked if I was planning to bring a camera and said again that he would be happy to talk. I suspect it was a combination of wanting to make me happy, to give me something I truly wanted, and a genuine desire to tell his story. Over the years, he often told us bits and pieces about old times, friends, trips, adventures and mishaps, but never in an organized manner. He would often reminisce when he was manic, eager to talk, and I would avoid interrupting his flow. A few times he even announced he was writing a book about his life. I specifically remember one title "Samuel (a pseudonym he often used) and Dikla (a girl's name with similar meaning to Alona, my mom's name)." I don't know what happened to it, but I've never actually seen it.

I arrived at my dad's kibbutz apartment in the late morning. It was a typical sunny December day in Israel. I knocked on the door and Joon opened it with a smile.

"Abba," he called over to my dad, using the Hebrew term for father, "your daughter is here."

In the video I shot that day, Dad is seated in his black leather armchair, wearing a faded sweatshirt over a red polo shirt. His hair and beard are completely white, but his mustache is yellow stained from smoking. An off-screen muted television flickers an occasional burst of blue light into the frame. The recording starts mid-conversation.

"Thanks to you I returned home," Dad says. "Thinking about it now, it was a good time. You prepared the house for me, and that's a big thing. You're the one who brought me home after two years."

"Yes, well, Dalia was working full time, she couldn't do it," I say.

"But you were the one who actually did it..."

"You didn't want to come home, you were afraid," I reminded him.

"Yes, it was a mistake. Are you all set with the camera? What else do you need?" he asks after a pause.

"Nothing, the camera is running."

"Should I take off my glasses?"

He turns off the TV, but we continue with small talk for a while, a comfortable back-and-forth about the extended family. Then, all of a sudden, he says, "Only two of us came back. Four of us went to the Six Day War but only two came back. Danny, who was Mom's first boyfriend before I took her from him, was shot right next to me. He was taking photos, and a sniper shot him, right through the camera."

He pauses, lost in thought, and I wait. In the kitchen you can hear the crackling sound of chicken frying in oil while Joon makes lunch.

"For me it all began in the Karameh battle," he jumps forward in time. "Thirty Israeli soldiers died there. A truck full of bodies. A colossal screw-up."

The door opens and Yair says he brought a replacement carafe for the coffee machine. The clip ends.

When the video resumes, I ask Dad again about Karameh.

"We arrived on reserve duty a month before, in February. The date it all began, for me, was March 21st. That's when it all started. It's a mystery, why it happened to me. You used to ask me about it, remember?"

"Yes, I think so," I say. And when he doesn't reply I continue, "I recall something, maybe you told me or someone else, that you were sent to collect a body, someone you knew, who was run over by a tank. Is that what happened?"

"Of course, yes, I had to pick up the remains and take them to the medical unit."

"Who was he? Did you know him?" I asked, trying to complete the fragments I remember into a coherent picture.

"He was one of us," Dad says, but doesn't elaborate. He reaches over and takes a pack of cigarettes from the shelf next to him. In a second Joon is there, waiting with the lighter.

"It's part of my confusion," Dad explains. "I have a hard time aiming the flame at the tip of the cigarette, it's even worse in the evenings."

Dad asks for a cup of instant soup and I get up to turn on the kettle, leaving the camera running. He remains in his seat, smoking. Watching the video now, I notice the hand holding the cigarette is shaking slightly, and he makes small involuntary movements with his head and mouth. I suspect these are the result of Tardive dyskinesia (TD), a side effect of anti-psychotic medications. When I return, Dad has turned on the TV and is watching a Steven Segal movie. He asks me to bring over an envelope with pictures that is on the shelf. For a moment the pattern of my shirt, wide stripes of white and gray, fills the frame, and the video ends.

A few days later I returned to visit with my family. In the photos I took that day, we are seated outside. Dad's makeshift sitting area is comprised of a low rectangular brown wooden table, scratched and peeling, standing on a poured concrete rectangle that serves as a flat base for it, but also as an anchor to a heavy metal chain that tethers the table to the ground. Two white plastic chairs and three green ones are arranged around it, slightly sinking into a layer of dry leaves that covers the dirt patio. The table is half covered with a Puzzle Track play set Dad bought for my kids. Next to it is an open bag of chocolate wafer cookies and a roll of toilet paper my dad uses as tissue.

Dad is wearing a blue, faded, zip up hoodie and gray sweat pants. In all the photos he is sitting in the same chair, in almost the same position, hands in his lap, his posture somewhat slumped. The rest of the family, my husband, my 13-year-old son and the 5-year-old twins are shifting between playing with the track set, eating, talking. In most of the images Dad's expression is alert and engaged, but my favorite photo of that day is a close-up of his face. His eyes are closed as he is holding a cigarette between two fingers and inhaling deeply. There is a calmness, a serenity in his expression. Is it happiness of being able to spend a good day interacting with the family or just the bliss of the nicotine rush hitting his brain after trying to refrain for longer than he is used to?

Despite some worsening of his leg pain, Dad came to the Bar-Mitzvah (we arranged for a wheelchair); the first family event he's been to in 9 years. He lit a candle and seemed happy to interact with the grandchildren and the other guests.

He remained in a good mood for several months. I continued to call him daily, and we talked about the family, movies, and current events. He liked to talk about local misfortunes and disasters. A deadly car crash, especially if it involved multiple casualties, a teenager who got electrocuted while attempting to hang a banner on an electric pole. I hated hearing about those things, but I let him tell me anyway. It's an Israeli thing, an obsession with news and disasters which I left behind when I moved to the U.S.

Around March, the phone calls began to shorten. In April my mother-in-law passed away and he couldn't gather the strength to go to the funeral with Dalia. In May there were days when he didn't pick up the phone at all. I came to visit again, this time by myself. We mostly watched TV together. By June, he had submerged into depression again.

Dad's mental and physical condition gradually deteriorated. One morning Joon found him on the floor. He'd fallen during the night and couldn't get up. We hired a night nurse. Around the same time, we realized that we could not get proper medical care for Dad on the kibbutz and decided that maybe we should look into homes for the elderly. By chance, while checking another facility, Dalia heard of a small home for people living with mental illness in a town not far from the kibbutz. It turned out that the woman running the place was someone my parents knew many years ago, which helped "sell" the move to my dad. While there, he received excellent care from a team that included a psychiatrist, social worker, physical therapist, and dedicated nurses and helpers. He was in better shape overall than he had been in previous years. My sister and her family visited often, as well as grandma and Yair. I visited a couple of times a year and even my mom and Dubi visited occasionally.

Dad stayed at "Beit Shalva" (loosely translated to "Tranquility Home") for less than two years before his fatal fall.

Patchwork

June 2015

The headstone unveiling service took place on a Friday afternoon. It was a small gathering, just my grandmother, Dad's siblings and their children, my sister, her family and me. As an opening, Dalia played a tune on a recorder. After that some of the cousins spoke. I told everybody about the interviews I'd conducted that week, with Yoav, Ginath and Roni and a bit about what they said about Dad.

We then went to Yair's house for refreshments and while everyone was catching up, Yair suggested my sister and I go to my dad's old apartment to see what was left of his belongings. My uncle had already cleared the apartment a while ago and turned it over to the kibbutz but had left some personal things packed in boxes in the shed.

We drove in separate cars to the other end of the kibbutz and parked in front of the ancient duplex. The new tenants had already placed a new sitting set on the gravel by the entrance and a large potted plant by the steps, but the shed remained as I remembered, a lean-to that my dad built by himself years ago, with a corrugated asbestos roof and sheath metal walls. The sun-bleached poles supporting it were originally brown but now flaked to a mottled shade of pink.

Yair unlocked the padlock on the door, and we entered the dark enclosure. I tried the light switch, but the single bare bulb hanging from the ceiling wasn't working anymore. So we waited for our eyes to adjust to the little sunlight that streamed between the walls and the roof, and after a couple of minutes, we were able to see the contents. There wasn't much, just four large cardboard boxes, taped haphazardly and covered with dust. We opened the first box, and the tang of cigarettes hit me—my dad's scent. As someone who never smoked, you'd think I'd hate that smell, but I don't. For me, the aroma of old cigarette fumes soaked into clothes, papers, or books is my dad's trademark. Every April, Dad used to mail me a book for my birthday, and every time the mail person gave me the box I knew it was from Dad by the faint cigarette scent that clung to the cardboard and had survived the shipment overseas. He once told me he took up smoking during his first hospital stay. There was just not much else to do, and everybody else smoked. Ever since, he had been a heavy smoker, easily burning through two packs a day.

In the boxes, we found framed photos of us and our kids that used to hang on the walls of his living room, now discolored and scratched. We looked through some old receipts, a photo-developing packet bursting with prints, a brown envelope with yellowing newspaper clips, my father's extensive collection of porn videos that we double bagged and deposited at the bottom of the trash container, and one large, framed portrait of my dad, with a woman we didn't recognize.

In the monochromatic print, the young couple is sitting in front of a white background, lit with professional portrait studio light. Dad is wearing a dark-colored polo shirt, his hair curly and light, his mustache a bit darker, smiling slightly and looking to the right of the photographer. She has short wavy hair, wearing a sleeveless polka dot shirt, and looking directly at the camera. Their heads leaning against each other. Lovers.

We gathered the things we wanted to keep and went back to my uncle's home. When we showed the photo of dad and the woman to Grandma, she said, "I don't know, but that must be Booka."

The name sounded remotely familiar—someone who my dad mentioned in the past, A girlfriend. Grandma didn't know much about her; in fact, she never met her, but she remembered she was from Tel-Aviv and had a young child from a previous marriage. She also thought she may have passed away already. They were a couple sometime after my parents' divorce and before the Yom Kippur war. She didn't know her last name but thought Booka was a nickname for Bruriah.

That evening, in my mom's kitchen, my sister and I looked again through the stuff we saved. I suggested we try and locate Booka or someone who knew her. Maybe through Facebook? I photographed the photo of the young couple with my phone, and while I composed a post, my sister pulled out the yellow newspaper clips from the envelope that was in one of the boxes.

My post went something like that:

> *Please share: I am looking for anybody who knew the woman in this photo (Booka or Bruriah) or the couple in the early 70's in Tel Aviv, or anybody who met Saul (He may have used another name) in Sinai after the Yom Kippur war.*

"Nits, you have to listen to this," my sister interrupted my scrolling down on my Facebook feed.

"What is it?"

"I think it's an article about Dad."

" About what?"

"About his mental illness. They made an effort to change identifying details, but it's clearly his story."

"Mark of Cain/ By Dina Ramaj" Dalia read the title with some formality.

"Depression is a form of internal paralysis. You want to end it.

I was there, but I didn't have the courage." Gilad, from a kibbutz in the South, was first hospitalized 20 years ago.

At the psychiatric hospital, they called it bipolar disorder. On the kibbutz, they say mental illness. But what difference does the label make for its victim, Gilad, from a kibbutz in the South?

When he was 23, an army veteran (elite unit), married, and a father, he experienced his first episode. The kibbutz reacted quickly. 4 men held him down and gave him a sedative. "I want you to write that they held me down and gave me an injection against my will at the doctor's order, although I did not fight with them." The next day he found himself tied to a bed in a high-security ward at a psychiatric hospital. This was 20 years ago.

Since then, he has been hospitalized repeatedly for prolonged periods and moved between different institutes and treatment methods. Today he is in remission, hoping for better times."

My sister stopped reading and handed me the paper clips to look at. Any identifying marks like the name of the publication or the date were cut away, but something about it was familiar.

"You know, I have a faint memory of an interview dad gave to the kibbutz paper," I said, referring to a biweekly newspaper supplement that was published and distributed to kibbutz members years ago. Or maybe still is. I wouldn't know.

"Did you know about the tying down?" My sister asked, and I shook my head.

We sat there for a while, Passing the paper between us, rereading passages. Again, I felt there was so much I didn't know about him.

While in Israel Mom also gave me a plastic bag with letters that she'd saved over the years. Some were from old pen pals, others were from my dad, sent to my mom when they were dating and later to me and my sister. I didn't have time to sort them out, but I took them home with me.

Our Facebook post got many Likes, hearts, encouraging comments, and shares, but no answers. My sister began to look for a Booka or Bruriah on Google and other websites to see if we could identify a person that matched the information we had and the photo.

Within the letters I brought with me, were a couple of letters written to Abigail, my dad's childhood classmate and friend from the kibbutz. Turns out she found those letters and sent them to my mom after my dad's funeral. In one of them, I was excited to find a reference to Booka. There was no date on the letter, and the stamp on the envelope was cut out (by an avid stamp collector?) So I could only guess from the content it was written sometimes in the mid-70's.

Abigail,

I do not have enough words to describe the importance of your visit and the happiness it brought me. (I often rejected the overused phrase "happiness," but this time, it is fitting). Following your visit, I again feel a connection to my home, and Ein Arava is my home after all, even if I distanced myself lately. Friends like you make me believe that despite all my "crimes," I will be able to build my home there again.

I had nine good months until recently, and I'm sorry if I didn't keep in touch, but Booka filled my world.

I'm about to tell you some personal things that I have not told anyone else because I don't trust anybody the way I trust you and Yossi.

Booka is an unbelievably brilliant woman, and I can only outthink her when I'm in controlled mania. And yet, after 3 months together, I was about to end our relationship because she tended to get upset, even hysterical. But then we found out she was pregnant, and the process of getting an abortion extended our relationship beyond the five-month mark.

Now, in "Mazra," I miss her a lot, the way a man longs for a woman. I don't mean to turn you into my confession priest, but I just want you to know how much I cared about her and how hard the separation is now that I'm in the hospital.

Abigail- please write often, and hopefully, I will be allowed to go on vacations to the kibbutz soon. Bye, S.

I texted my sister, I FOUND SOME INFORMATION ABOUT BOOKA, and she texted back, I HAVE SOMETHING TOO. TALK LATER?

She called me from the car on her way back from work. As a working mother of 5, driving was her only free time.

"I think I may have found her," she said without any preliminaries, "or at least a Booka of the right age, born in 44, like Dad. I mean, not her, but her full name and family tree on the MyHeritage website. There is no picture, but there's the name of her son; I'll try to see if he's on Facebook or Linkedin or something."

I gave her a summary of the letter. That they were a couple for 5 months, the pregnancy and abortion.

We hoped that if we find her son, he will remember Dad or will be able to connect us with other family or friends who have recollections of the relationship.

The next day, when I woke up in the morning, I had a message from Dalia. She managed to connect with the son on LinkedIn and speak to him, but he doesn't remember our dad, and more importantly, said the woman in the photo is not his mom. I was disappointed. We were back at square one, or not even because we haven't found any other Booka or Bruriah that fit the profile.

I had some time that day, so I went back to read through my dad's letters. In one of the envelopes, I found a faded photo of a woman I didn't recognize. There was nothing written on the print or the envelope. I sent a picture to my sister and asked her to check with Booka's son if that might be his mom.

The search had an anticlimactic ending. Booka's son confirmed that the second photo was of his mom, but he still had no recollection of Dad, possibly because he was too young at the time. He connected my sister with his mom's best friend, but she didn't remember Dad either. We also never found out who the woman in the other photograph was.

For a little while, I hoped to uncover a big colorful centerpiece for our patchwork quilt, but it turned out that the fading of time and memory bleached my dad›s and Booka's romance almost in its entirety, leaving just a few shades of pen-blue longings and a yellowing Polaroid as evidence.

And so it joins the other pieces. Some of them brighter but very small, others dark with pain or moth-eaten with missing information. Most of them as pallid as that last one.

But still, with every box we open, every old friend we speak to, every document we unearth, the tapestry expands, and slowly, a likeness of my dad is revealed, smelling faintly of cigarettes.

An article published in 1986-7

Mark of Cain by Dina Ramaj

Depression is a form of internal paralysis. You want to end it. I was there, but I didn't have the courage." Gilad, from a kibbutz in the South, was first hospitalized 20 years ago.

At the psychiatric hospital, they call it bipolar disorder. On the kibbutz they say mental illness. But what difference does the label make for its victim, Gilad, from a kibbutz in the South?

When he was 23, an army veteran (an elite unit), married and a father, came the first episode. The kibbutz reacted quickly. 4 men held him down and gave him a sedative. "I want you to write that they held me down and injected me against my will at the doctor's order, although I did not fight with them." -and took him under sedation to the regional psychiatrist. The next day he found himself tied to a bed in a high-security ward at a psychiatric hospital. This was 20 years ago.

Since then, he has been hospitalized repeatedly for prolonged periods and moved between different institutes and treatment methods. Today he is in remission, hoping for better times.

Gilad is well aware of his situation and knows that there is no cure yet for his condition. In his calm appearance - strong and tanned like you'd expect any man born on a kibbutz, there are no clues or signs that will testify to the disease eating away at his soul. In our conversation that took place during a respite (He has not been hospitalized in 10 months), he told me his story and demonstrated a vast knowledge of mental illnesses and psychiatric medicine.

His story begins with a happy childhood in the kibbutz, Successful school years and army service, early marriage, and assimilation in the kibbutz life. In that chapter of his life, there was no evidence of the disease lurking inside "It's genetic, in my family for generations, there are other relatives like me." Looking back, he does remember periods of melancholia, once after a first love heartbreak and once again in the army. Still, it seemed to be within the normal range. It all changed after a traumatic event in the military. Gilad seemingly recovered from the incident, however shortly after, when he returned to the kibbutz and was put in charge of one of the kibbutz's operations, he got stressed and had another mental breakdown. His behavior became rough and stormy, his reactions volatile. The kibbutz was aware of the changes, and when it was found out that he also spent the nights joyriding with a young woman, they decided to take steps.

"I can't blame them," he says. "But that's when I realized the level of ignorance and intolerance. They tied me up to take me to the doctor even though I wasn't violent, I didn't struggle. They did it at the hospital, too, without provocation, just in case you wouldn't rile up or interrupt the nurse's sleep… Doctors like these things safe and away from them."

Acceptance

On that first ride to the hospital, the doctor told Gilad: "Sir, you are ill. Take those pills and go home until we decide on a treatment." The kibbutz started monitoring him. He became irate, and claimed he was attacked. He took a car and drove to the police station to file a complaint. A few minutes later, the kibbutz director arrived as well. He pulled the policemen aside to confer.

Later, Gilad will learn that there will always be someone else that will try to explain his situation like he wasn't even present. He was again tied with a rope and taken to the doctor. "I wanted others to see what they were doing to me. That I'm not fighting back." In the hospital, the doctor suggested an injection "just to calm you down." Gilad agreed and immediately fell asleep. "That was a lie, an easy way to hospitalize me. I woke up the next day in the stinkiest hospital in the country. Behind a facade of lawns and gardens, they kept in the back rooms chronic patients that any resemblance between them and human-beings is incidental. I will never forget that nightmare."

Gilad stayed there for a week, in a closed ward, until he managed to escape. He found a car and drove toward home but got stuck. He called the kibbutz for help. The director appeared again with some muscular guys. "They didn't even say hello, asked how I was, brought someone from the family with them…»

It's been many years since then, but Gilad is still troubled by that memory. He understands that he's sick and does not argue with the need for occasional hospitalization. Still, he feels that he was treated as if he ceased to feel, as if he was no longer worthy of sympathy.

From that horrible place, Gilad was transferred to a better hospital in Jerusalem. Following 2 months of hospitalization, first in a secure unit and later in an open one, he returned to the kibbutz and his family, but the previous events caused him shame and embracement. He hoped to avoid the people who were involved, wished to run away from the stigma, but eventually decided to forgive and stay. "It's a recurring theme with me, giving in, surrendering, either because of the family or for other reasons or maybe that's who I am, all bark and no bite."

Worthless person

Intermittently, he experienced depression and mania, "High," as he calls it. Another hospitalization and back to the kibbutz. Then a divorce, "I understand her, I knew it was coming, I expected it."

Gilad decided to leave the kibbutz. "I felt uneasy, living on the kibbutz with the mentally ill label. It's not the hospitalizations but the shenanigans that preceded it. I had no chance of actively participating in the community again, of serving on comity, of being trusted with any responsibility. I was confined to a life-long position of a manual laborer. kibbutz members didn't stop by to say hi, didn't join me at the Dining Room table or at the "club." I wanted to be anonymous, to rid of my Mark of Cain."

His time in the city was fraught with mishaps. He tried to make a living as a driver but was negligent, involved in traffic violations, and minor accidents. He didn't have permanent lodging, and if it wasn't for the packages of food his parents sent him, he would have starved. In one of his visits to the kibbutz he took his child with him without the mother's knowledge. Until the child was found at a friend's home, he raised a serious alarm in the kibbutz.

A year later, while he was again in a volatile state, he visited the kibbutz. Some members suggested that he be hospitalized. "I didn't fight them this time, I knew already that it wasn't my choice, I call it Passive Objection. Maybe I felt already that it was time to get treatment."

His stay at the mental institute ended again with an escape. He stole a car and drove 100 miles per hour, "I was mentally out of balance, I thought I was being chased." The vehicle flipped over and was destroyed. It was only a miracle that Gilad was unharmed. At a judge's order, he was hospitalized at a secure institute for several years. Most of the time, he suffered from depression. Hopeless, he was afraid that he would remain there for the rest of his life.

"Depression is a form of internal paralysis," explains Gilad, "everything is down, all the functions including the brain. I would sit all day and digest my past and tell myself that I'm worthless and have no future. Only bad memories surface. It's a complete lack of self-esteem. I would tell myself that I deserve it, that I'm nothing. It's a horrible feeling. You want to end it. I didn't end it because I didn't have the courage."

Back to the kibbutz

Memories of that time infuriate him: "I burned away my best years there. Did anybody care? I was treated with various medications and electric shocks, That's the routine over there. They do it for no good reason. They don't know how to treat it, they don't even bother to see the patients."

Coming back to the kibbutz was a sign of progress, however limited, in his treatment. During quiet times Gilad returned to work but did not resume social life. He stayed for long days in his parent's apartment, barely communicating. His family had to deal with the awkward situation, a son who doesn't talk and spreads glum all around him. "I never spoke to my parents about it, but I know that my condition was a heavy burden. When I was at the mental institute, my mother came to visit every Saturday. She had to get up early, beg for someone to drive her to the main road, take a taxi there and then walk the long entrance to the hospital, carrying heavy bags with supplies for me. I would sit with her in silence. I'm sure that people pity my parents, thinking to themselves: Look where my son is and look at yours."

And then the cycle starts again, From depression to temporary normalcy and then to mania again. "First signs of mania are less sleep, overactivity, a need to talk a lot, a kind of compensation for everything missing during the depression. There's excitement about work, a passion for building, or organizing things, for creating. It's self-love and love of others, It's extreme happiness."

The mania, or "hi" can be controlled with medications but not the depression, which tends to arrive in the winter. "It's a horrible feeling. You know it's coming, but you can't stop it."

No way out

When he was transferred to another mental institute, Gilad encountered a better level of care by trained professionals using more progressive methods. No more closed units of 45 patients together in one room, but instead a modern, open building with a calm, warm atmosphere. Most patients were there for short periods and then returned home. The new approach helped Gilad, his condition improved, and he learned to "live with it" as much as possible.

However, psychiatric treatment, even an excellent one, is not enough. The recovery of a mentally ill person depends mainly on his home and his environment. As long as he lives on the kibbutz in solitude, he is unlikely to overcome the self-doubts and shame that torment him. Weary of rejection, he confines himself to seclusion, and as a result, his day-to-day functioning suffers.

The kibbutz today shows better sensitivity to those considered "different." There's a willingness to offer assistance and support and to create the best conditions for recovery. Gilad meets regularly with a social worker and is assigned a liaison, a kibbutz member from whom he can request assistance, and who aids him if he encounters untoward work-related or social situations.

Five years ago, Gilad got involved with a woman, and she decided to come live with him in the kibbutz. She supports him through the darkest times and gives him a renewed desire to live." She always encourages me to try and get out of the hospital, she is very special." He has no secrets from her, she knows when "it happens," and she also knows it will eventually pass. She stays by him when he's depressed, and he credits her for his current happiness.

The kibbutz is a close-knit community. While it could be protective and supportive, it can also be a hurdle to the recovery of the mentally ill. "There's nowhere to hide. Everybody knows about you. There will always be someone who will know better than you what is right for you. I'm in the hands of others who decide for me, who can force me to be hospitalized. Every time I go for a follow-up at the hospital, I know it could end in hospitalization. It's enough that someone from the kibbutz will call and say something. Maybe someone interpreted something I did to mean that I'm not well. I'm constantly worried that someone's bias will decide my fate. Once and again, I feel that I want to leave everything, disconnect from the kibbutz, just be myself with no liaisons or guardians.

Epilogue

Six months after my dad passed away, I got a message from Eli, a camera person I met briefly in New York. He told me that someone he knows is looking for a videographer to document a project in Uganda and asked if I'd be interested in hearing more.

A day or two later, I spoke on the phone with Raffael, an Israeli artist. He explained that he'd been working on an art project with refugee children in Africa and was planning to travel to Uganda again soon. He said he was looking for a videographer to document the work he was doing.

Raffael spoke quickly, spewing terms and names as I furiously scribbled notes on a piece of paper, trying to capture as much information as possible. He told me about his project, mixing anecdotes and grandiose plans. He wanted to take a group of refugees from Kampala, who'd been deported from Israel (I wasn't aware that the Israeli government deported refugees to Africa) to a Jewish village in Uganda (I didn't know there were Ugandan Jews). He also hoped to celebrate Hanukah together, choreograph a dance, and have the refugees teach the locals Hebrew, hoping that perhaps some of them could become Hebrew teachers in the community after graduating High School. He didn't have money to pay me; he barely had money for the trip, and he also said he wasn't exactly sure where the village was or how to get the children there.

Halfway through our conversation, I began to feel uncomfortable. Raffael's excitement reminded me of my father when he was becoming manic. In my experience, plans made during bouts of mania never came to fruition. Was I getting excited for nothing? Or worse, was I going to fly all the way to Uganda just to turn around?

Before he hung up, Raffael promised to send me a link with further information and we agreed to speak again in a few days.

I sat at my desk looking at my notes. I googled "Abuyudaya," the Jewish community of Uganda, and the village Namutumba that Raffael was planning to visit. I found no images of the village online, but there was a Wikipedia page about the Abuyudaya with a fascinating story about its origins. Next, I checked out the link Raffael sent me. It was an incredibly touching TV story about the group of deported refugee children Raffael mentioned.

The project seemed exciting and worthy, yet I was still feeling uneasy. Part of it was the challenge of filming in such conditions by myself. I wasn't even sure what the conditions would be. But there was something else.

Eventually, I stopped the research and thought through what was bothering me. I was unable to shake off the feeling that Raffael was not reliable. Should I just say no, I'm sorry, can't do it, and forget about it?

I finally gathered the courage and called Eli. What should I say? That Raffael sounded manic? Based on what? So I began in a roundabout approach, something along the lines of, "I spoke to Raffael. He sounds very nice and he's a fascinating character, but is he okay? How well do you know him?"

To my surprise, Eli understood right away what I was asking. "Yes," he said, "Raffael does have a history of a mood disorder, but he is one hundred percent reliable and always completes his grandiose ideas."

I was relieved and continued to prepare for the trip. I also looked up the price of changing my flight back and the availability of reasonable hotels near the airport—just in case no one picked me up.

The trip to Uganda was interesting despite being extremely stressful at times. The refugee teens were inspiring, and the Jewish community was fascinating and welcoming. Raffael and I managed to get along most of the time, although his insistence on his ideas and priorities often left me scrambling to set up the camera in a hurry or cut an interview short.

When I returned home, I planned to send him the material I filmed and part ways, but a couple of months later, he called to ask if I could help him edit a short film about our trip to Uganda to be screened in an exhibit at a San Diego museum. Reluctant at first, I agreed to work with him again. The exhibition in San Diego in the summer of 2016 was a success, and the short film I edited with my friend Liki Tapuach was well received.

During one of our numerous phone calls, Raffael mentioned the story of how he became an artist. As he tells it, in 1995, he suffered severe depression and attempted suicide. While hospitalized in a psychiatric hospital, he found a pile of screws and began asking other patients and staff if they were their "missing screws." He ended up sculpting a 10-foot-tall screw out of foam core and fiberglass and taking it on a journey around the world. I remember thinking to myself that this could have been a great film if only I were there to film it.

Meanwhile, I continued to work on my "Dad" project. During my summer visit to Israel, I conducted more interviews and attempted to unearth more written material for details or to confirm vague memories.

At a documentary film class at the School of Visual Arts in Manhattan, I discussed the idea. When asked about the visual material that I intend to use, I admitted that other than interviews, I don't have any footage. I said I thought of recreating scenes in an artistic, blurry, minimalistic style. I still remember the instructor's mocking tone when he repeated the idea to the class to ask their opinion.

A few months after the San Diego show, I got a call from Raffael. He asked me if I would be interested in making a documentary about his journey with the screw. I replied that I thought it was a great story but wondered out loud what visuals I could use since it had happened years ago.

To my surprise, Raffael told me that he and others had filmed throughout the journey and had many hours of footage on video cassettes. After viewing a sample of the material and hearing more details, we signed a contract that gave me the rights to the story.

The process of locating the material, converting the video cassettes to digital files, and learning about Raffael's story details dragged on. I planned to begin interviews with Raffael and his family in the spring of 2020. We all know what happened then.

A few weeks into the Covid quarantine, I got an e-mail about an online memoir writing class. Since I could not progress with my film project, and there was not much else to do (other than experiment with baking my own bagels), I signed up. That was the beginning of the book you have just read.

At the same time, through hours of phone interviews with Raffael, I realized that his story had many parallels to my dad's.

So, instead of making a film about my dad, I produced and directed the movie "My Missing Screw," about Raffael and his family, and the interviews I filmed became the basis for this book.

In respect of the privacy of my family and friends, I have changed the names of most of the people and places in the book.